CLEVEDON ....
CLUBS, CAKES, QUARRIES & CASH

Group of Clevedon businessmen at a monthly meeting at the Oak room Café during 1943/44
Photo : courtesy of Mrs Joan Hack (nee Pallent)

Published by the Clevedon Civic Society

2002

ISBN 1 901 084 35 3

Contents

			Page
FOREWORD		Julia Elton C.C.S. President.	3
INTRODUCTION		Rob Campbell, Local History Group Chairman	4
CLUBS	CLEVEDON TOWN A. F. C.	Douglas Hand	6
	GUIDING IN CLEVEDON	Mary House	9
	THE CLEVEDON AMATEUR SWIMMING CLUB	Laurie Eager	18
	RIFLE CLUB	Mervyn Potter	26
	THE PIER TRUST	Austin Davis	33
	PERFORMING ARTS CLUBS —		
	LIGHT OPERA CLUB	Gordon Lawrence	40
	CLEVEDON PLAYERS	Alan Cooper	42
	COMEDY CLUB	Val Vella	46
	GILBERT & SULLIVAN SOCIETY	Roger Carroll	48
CAKES	HALES BAKERY	Roy Girling	51
QUARRIES	CLEVEDON'S QUARRIES	Roy Girling with Jane & Derek Lilly	63
CASH	BANKING IN CLEVEDON	Christopher Norrish	70
FOOTNOTE		Peggy Tigwell	75
ACKNOWLEDGEMENTS			76

Photograph on Frontispiece

Back Row	W. Mangham? Mercury	T. Pallent Hales	T. Roynon Boot Factory	—?—	H. Willcocks Clevedon Eng.	D. Hawkins Builders
Middle Row	—?—	A. Binding Binding & Payne	H. Lock W & T Lock Bath	T.Miller Millcross	T. Trask Beatrice Engineering	H. Pryce Weeches
Front Row	T. May Brick Works & Laundry	—?—	A. W. Hand Boot Factory	S. Bennett Labour Exchange	E. Dunn Clevedon & Yatton Gas	O. Binding Binding & Payne

If you are able to fill in any of the missing names please contact the editor.

Foreword

The Civic Society's new book is largely concerned with Clevedon at play. What makes it so absorbing, however, is that it conjures up life in 20th century Clevedon and activities that many of us know about or will even have participated in. Local history, after all, begins yesterday.

A guidebook of 1905/6 lists what were clearly well-established clubs for golf, cricket and lawn tennis, though oddly doesn't mention the Clevedon Town Football Club, which, we learn from this book, began playing much earlier, in 1880. The Clevedon Amateur Swimming Club was only founded in 1929 but developed out of the earlier Clevedon Aquatic Sports Club. Many of us will recognise the names of friends and acquaintances in the lists of winners of the Long Swim. The Rifle Club was formed much later, in the wake of the last war, and its members built their own clubhouse, truly a remarkable example of local enterprise. The performing arts clubs, which make an outstanding contribution to life in the town, were also founded after the last war but although most people will have attended performances of the Light Opera and Comedy Clubs or of the Clevedon Players and the Gilbert & Sullivan Society, how many know about their histories?

Two further leisure activities are included here. The Girl Guide movement got under way in Clevedon in 1913 and remarkably is still going strong, while the story of the Pier supporters and the Pier Trust is brought up to date with the triumphant completion of the Pier restoration after years of unflagging local support. All this abundant energy has clearly been fuelled and sustained by another remarkable local enterprise. How many generations of local sportsmen, actors, musicians, guides and activists have consumed Farmhouse, Banbury or Sultana cakes or jam tarts and swiss rolls produced by Frank Hale? This is a story of which all Clevedonians can be proud and is here told in detail for the first time. The Civic Society is, as always, concerned with all aspects of our history and there is something for everyone to remember and enjoy in this book.

Julia Elton

President - Clevedon Civic Society

Introduction

With the growth in population of the town came the proliferation of clubs and societies. The intricate weave between work and social commitments is further explored in this the latest offering from the Civic Society Local History Group. There are over one hundred Clubs, Societies and Leisure Organisations listed in the latest Clevedon Directory and some of them have a history which spans over one hundred years. A contact was made with a number of Group Secretaries asking if any of their members could contribute in any way. The results of their efforts can be read under the heading of **CLUBS.**

1928 saw the opening of Clevedon's largest ever employer "Hales Home Bakeries". Mention was made that its recorded history was rather sparse. A start was made by tracking down ex-employees and what started as a trickle turned into an avalanche of memorabilia, enough to write a book, let alone a chapter. Sorting through we gained quite a taste for it, the resulting chapter is entitled **CAKES.**

One of our readers noticed in the last book that we had in mind a chapter on quarrying, he put pen to paper and provided his reminiscences of 65 years ago. This initiated a look into all the quarrying that has taken place within the town and, with the unparalleled assistance from our two renowned local historians, the **QUARRIES** chapter evolved.

What makes the world go round? In addition to all the people involved and the hard work put in by many, we must have money, so a look back into the local banking business can be found under the heading **CASH.**

If after reading the chapters you feel that your group has a further story that is worth telling then please contact us and with your help we shall be able to publish a further volume. The Clevedon Civic Society Local History Group wishes to thank all who have contributed in any way, but special mention must go to Roy Girling who has acted as collator and editor of all the material furnished.

So please read on, the following pages will illuminate many of the fascinating facts from Clevedon's colourful past.

Rob Campbell
Local History Group Chairman

CLUBS

Clevedon Town A.F.C. — History

Guiding in Clevedon 1913 - 2000

Clevedon Amateur Swimming Club

Clevedon Rifle Club 1950

Clevedon Pier, 1990 - 2001

Clevedon Performing Arts Clubs:
    Clevedon Light Opera Club
    The Clevedon Players
    Clevedon Comedy Club
    Gilbert & Sullivan Society

Clevedon Town A.F.C. — History

Clevedon commenced playing Association Football in 1880 at the local cricket ground on Dial Hill. They became founder members of the Western League in 1892 and finished fifth for two seasons in succession. Then followed calamity in 1894/95 finishing bottom. (P22. W1 . D1. lost 20. F23. A 136 Points 3) and they returned to junior football.

The commencement of season 1895/96 saw the arrival of a new secretary, Mr. Herbert George Hand. This was the beginning of a 100 year long association by this family, he was followed by his son, A.W.Hand (Bill) and then grandson Douglas. Douglas retired as President in 1995.

When Herbert Hand took over in 1895 he already had football administrative experience in Bristol. He had helped form the Black Arabs A.F.C. who became Eastville Rovers and finally Bristol Rovers as we know them today.

The Hand family moved to Clevedon in 1892 and worked for J.H.Woodington Ltd, Boot Works at St.George, Bristol and moved to Clevedon on the construction of the Boot Works at the bottom of Strode Road, now, AMPEP. Mr Woodington eventually had factories at Chesham, Bucks, Drogheda Nr. Dublin and a tannery at Mardyke, Hotwells. This was destroyed in the Bristol blitz in 1941, the same night as the Bristol City stand was destroyed.

Herbert Hand retired in 1912 and became the Club's first life member. The Scroll

Clevedon Town Amateur Football Club - Season 1923/24
Photo - courtesy of Bert Price

Quarries & Cash

hangs in the boardroom today. Amongst other early photographs one shows the team with shin guards outside their stockings and Somerset County Players with caps. One of the team members was a local poacher and missed games because of prison sentences.

In 1895 Clevedon moved to the Teignmouth Road Ground. The main entrance at that time was from Old Street, through Shopland's Sawmills, where one walked on planks to avoid mud and puddles of water. Another entrance, narrow footpath only, was from Parnell Road and then a walk alongside the Weston, Clevedon and Portishead Light Railway lines. The railway initials being - W.C.& P. which caused amusement to visitors.

Mr. A. W. Hand became Secretary in 1918 following war service and served for 50 years. Clevedon then played in the Bristol and District League, were Bristol Suburban League Champions 1925/26, 1927/28 and 1928/29; Somerset Senior League Champions 1936/37 and Bristol Charity League Champions 1937/38 and 1940/44.

At the outbreak of war in 1939 Clevedon joined the Weston-super-Mare League which was very strong because of international footballers at R.A.F. Locking. Clevedon had help from the East Yorks Regiment stationed in Clevedon. With several League players in their ranks the Club was very good and local players home on leave were found a game so they always brought their boots home with them.

Clevedon had considerable success in the war period, winning the League 1939/40, 1943/44, 1944/45, WSM Charity Cup 1940/41 and 1941/42. WSM Knock out Cup 1939/40, Weston-super-Mare Hospital Cup 1939/40.

At the end of the 1939/45 war, Clevedon re-joined the Western League.

The third generation of the Hand family, Doulas Hand became Assistant Secretary in 1946 following demobilisation from the R.A.F.

In 1947 Clevedon played in front of their biggest attendance ever, 10,000 at Penydarren Park, Merthyr in the F.A.Cup. At that time, football was in its hey-day, drawing large crowds everywhere and Merthyr were top of the Southern League. The team went by train and supporters part way by paddle steamer from Clevedon to Cardiff pier. What a performance the team put up, losing narrowly 2-1. After being reduced to 10 men, Rodney Cowdery breaking his leg after 20 minutes play. No substitutes in those days. The ovation given to Clevedon at the final whistle was very moving.

In 1948, Mr. Bill Hand negotiated the purchase of the ground for £450 and later sold to a developer for over a £1,000,000. It was about this time Clevedon commenced a wonderful run of success in the F. A. Amateur Cup reaching the rounds proper 8 times in the space of 13 seasons. Meeting such teams as Billingham Synthonia Recreation, two nights at the Grand Hotel, Bristol for them: Wimbledon, now a Premier Division Club and F. A. Cup Winners, a one all draw at Clevedon and losing 4-3 after extra time in the replay.

Other clubs were Ilford, Harwich and Parkstone, Pegasus at Iffley Road, Oxford where Roger Bannister ran the first 4 minute mile a few weeks earlier.

Briggs Sports arrived as champions of the Spartan League, but Clevedon won 4 nil with only about 25% possession. Goal keeper Jim Carey was carried shoulder high off the pitch. The record home gate was against Bath City on September 15th, 1951 when 2,300 witnessed a 3-1 victory for Bath. They brought many supporters on special trains and coaches, Clevedon had a railway station in those days. The success in the Cups was not reflected in their League form and they dropped into the Bristol Premier Combination in 1958. They returned to the Western League in 1973. In 1974 they turned professional with Ray Mabbutt, ex. Bristol Rovers, their first paid player. Ray is the father of Gary, the former England International and Tottenham Hotspur Captain. In season 1992/3, one hundred years after being founder members, Clevedon won the League without losing a game. *(Played 38. Won 34, drawn 4 lost nil. F137. A23 points 106)*. This was their first season at their new ground and named "The Hand Stadium" in recognition of the family's involvement. This is one of the best non-league grounds in the west of England and in 1993/4 the team gained promotion to the Beazer Homes League.

Financial problems again occurred and the Club was initially saved by one group of business men and after another crisis by the present owners, the Bradshaw Group. They have given the Club stability to the extent that in season 1998/9 they won the Dr. Martin's Midlands Division title after switching divisions at the end of 1997/8 and also the Somerset Premier Cup. They now compete in the Premier Division, the highest level ever achieved in their long history.

On adjoining pitches, Clevedon Ladies Football play and on another with Astra Turf provides hockey for Clevedon and Yatton Men and Ladies Clubs. Schoolboy football in the town is well catered for with the Town and United Clubs running teams from under 7 years of age upwards. Girls also compete up to a certain age.

Season 1999/2000, saw local football club, Clevedon United commence their first eleven Somerset League Matches at "The HAND". Their ambition being Screwfix Western League Football, which the facilities at the stadium would provide.

The Bradshaw Group have transformed the Club House into thriving business facilities, including conferences, seminars, business meetings, exhibitions, training and presentations. Facilities for social function include anniversaries, wedding parties, engagement and birthday parties, disco and cabaret evenings, sports and social club dinners and club A.G.M's. In 1999, the Bradshaw Group purchased the Equestrian Centre, (next door) one of the top 5 in the country. This immediately provided the football club with a much larger parking area for their top fixtures.

This Club History was produced by Mr. Douglas Hand, grandson of Herbert George Hand and given to the Local History Group for publication.

Guiding in Clevedon 1913 - 2000

Robert Baden-Powell published a book called Scouting for Boys in 1908 and boys and girls took up Scouting. In 1909 the first Boy Scout Rally was held at Crystal Palace. The attendance of girls at the Rally made it apparent that they were here to stay and so in 1910 The Girl Guide association was formed with Agnes Baden-Powell, sister of the Founder as President.

In 1912 Robert Baden-Powell married Olave Soames - who in 1916 was to become the World Chief Guide - and the first Guide handbook was printed, called How Girls Can Help To Build Up The Empire.

> **GIRL GUIDES FOR CLEVEDON**   (Clevedon Mercury 7th June 1913)
>
> *At a well attended meeting at the Public Hall on Monday evening, under the chairmanship of Colonel Montgomery, the idea of taking up locally the Baden-Powell Girl Guide Movement was heartily entered into.*

The Public Hall is long gone but the Guide movement is still going strong!

Later that year 2 companies were formed A year later 3 companies were registered, including one at the YMCA and another at the Girls' Friendly Society.

The first ever training camp for guiders was held in Clevedon during 1914 and two years later big displays were held at Clevedon Court.

"Guides at Clevedon Court"

During these early years of Guiding various amusing stories survive which I feel should be shared!

One evening the Guides built a bridge across the River Yeo behind the Cinema and asked their Captain to be the first across. As she gingerly lifted her long skirt and put one buttoned boot upon the bridge it was washed away by flood water as someone higher up the river opened the sluice gates!

One mother was forced to purchase, and pluck, a goose as her Guide daughter insisted that as she was a member of the 'Goose Patrol' she had to wear a Goose feather in her hat!

(It was in this period that Guiders wore large cocks feathers in the side of their hats to denote their rank)

The Junior section (8-11yrs) started in 1914 and were originally called Rosebuds, this changed to Brownies the following year. Clevedon's first Brownie Pack was formed in 1918, they had to make their own knitted hats as part of their initial test.

During the next 6 years Guiding flourished in the town and surrounding districts, several camps for blind and deaf children were held at Valetta in Bay Road. The Chief Guide, Lady Baden-Powell visited the town. Camps were held for Guides on Walton Hill behind the castle and a favourite place for camp fires was in the Old Quarry off Holly Lane and on Strawberry Hill (then known as Bella Vista). Clevedon became a popular place for summer camps and girls from far and wide spent time here to enjoy the 'bracing sea airs'.

During these early years Guide officers had to pass an examination set by the 'Clevedon Board of Examiners'. It is to be noted that recommendations were sent to the Town Council from the Guide committee regarding the running of the town, obviously a force to be reckoned with in those days!

In 1922 the Girl Guide Association was granted a Royal Charter of Incorporation.

Foxlease, Lyndhurst, Hants, is known to all Guides as Princess Mary House because it was endowed with wedding present money from the Princess Royal. This is the nearest Training Centre for Guiders in this area and loved and visited still today.

Rangers started in Clevedon in 1926, there were now 177 girls in the movement. There were no 'open' units at this time, all being either attached to schools or churches. The Guide committee had grown so large it was decided to split the meetings, this, probably, when the Local Association came into being here (Supporters Group). 1928 saw the first Division split - Clevedon and Portishead became one Division and Weston-s-Mare another. The guide movement was growing all over the country and new Divisions needing to be formed to make them manageable sizes. Of course Division Commissioners did not have the car to rely on as they do today. Clevedon Guides received recognition from the Government for work carried out during the General Strike.

The 1930s saw many changes - local Bye-laws were discarded when the Association's Policy, Organisations and

QUARRIES & CASH

Rules (POR) became every Guider's 'Bible'! Closer co-operation with the Scout association developed - we are after all from the same coin so to speak! Uniforms changed - not so that you would notice today! A Scout Jamboree was held in 1939 on the land where Clevedon Community School stands today - it is to be noted that the Guides did the cooking! At this time there were 24 Guide Leaders in Clevedon, this was soon to change as War was declared and Guiders went off to Serve the Empire in ways Baden-Powell had not foretold.

The Guides War Effort in Clevedon got under way with all speed, they collected waste paper, picked nettles(!) and knitted for the troops. One company chopped and sold firewood and raised £8 for the Spitfire fund. Guides and Scouts collected 113 tons of waste paper between 1940 and 1942 despite one nasty occasion when a mouse ran up a Guide's leg as she was jumping in a sack to pack it more tightly! During the war Guides knitted a total of 725 articles; pullovers, helmets, socks, gloves and scarves for the forces. They distributed notices and leaflets, collected rose hips and chestnuts and over £500 was raised for various war funds.

To add to the misery Lord Baden-Powell died in 1941. More than half of the Guiders joined the forces, land army or did factory work. Some units closed, some merged and meetings were held on Saturday and Sunday afternoons because of the blackout.

However where there's a will there's a way and Guiding continued with everyone truly lending a hand and helping each other.

In 1942 the Guide International Service was formed (GIS), for selection and training of Guiders for relief work after the war. Many Guiders did incredible work in countries that had been occupied. Although set up by Headquarters in London, Clevedon was keen to support and fund raising events were held to help support this.

1946 saw numbers grow to 300 in Clevedon, but with less paperwork luckily as there was still a shortage. OUT went large brimmed hats and IN came the beret. These post war years saw Guiding - and other youth movements - grow in popularity. There was a challenge to do everything offered in the programme and to do it well. The Queen's Guide Award became the highest achievement for Guides and became accepted as a mark of excellence. The Guide movement as a whole became more structured in its set up, more efficient at coping with the increased numbers and providing necessary training and help.

Locally this was reflected in Guider's willingness to attend trainings and give up their holidays to take Guides to camp. More supporters and leaders were required, the need is still there today. Overseas links and camps became possible.

The Town Council was keen to show interest and Guides were regularly asked to help at local events and to provide entertainment such as Country Dancing on the sea front! New units sprang up, including Sea and Air Rangers, girls were keen to become part of an international association with opportunities for leisure activities which were fun and educational giving them a sense of purpose.

By 1948 there were 5 Brownie Packs, 5 Guide and 2 Ranger companies. Numbers are not recorded but if each unit were full and including Guiders there would have been approximately 400 members. Lady Elton was President of Clevedon District and Clevedon Court was a favourite venue for Guiding occasions and camp trainings. Events included adventure camps, swimming competitions, Pageants, ceremonies for Empire Day, Church services for Thinking Day and Carol services. Girls wore their uniform with pride on every possible occasion, especially to school on a notable day.

During the late '40s the District continued to grow and as to-day there were difficulties in finding Guiders and Commissioners - dedicated women continued to hold units together with very little help. The Clevedon Trefoil Guild was formed, for members of the movement who had made their promise, but were not in active Guiding. The Local Association - supporters of the aims and objectives of the Guide Association - helped in many ways at this time and had more input into the running of the District than in later years, their role at this time was not merely fund raising but active support to the Guiders. It was during this time that the dividing of Clevedon into 2 Districts was first considered but this was not to happen until nearly 20 years later.

The 1950s saw Guiding's appeal to girls and young women increase considerably, their numbers became quite powerful in local youth related decision making all round the country, District Councils - Clevedon included - invited their participation.

Two Clevedon Guiders were invited by the Clevedon Chamber of Trade to attend meetings to look into the viability of a Public Hall.

The Arts and Outdoor activities were much in the forefront of the Guide programme at this time - Plays and Concerts were put on regularly - and well attended by the general public as well as relations. Church and other parades complete with Scout bands were held whenever a suitable opportunity offered. Sports days and Swimming galas played a big part in the summer programme as did hiking and overnight patrol camps - unhappily not considered a safe activity for girls on their own today.

Summer camp was the highlight, everyone wanted to go, and most had a wonderful and unforgettable time. This was before the time of sophisticated camp equipment that girls to-day expect (like hair dryers and flush toilets)! However the experience of camp 'before modernisation' was unforgettable and was looked forward to from year to year.

The high profile, which Guiding enjoyed at this time and into the 1960s, was reflected in the reports in newspapers. The Clevedon Mercury faithfully reported Annual General meetings almost word for word! Any activity had photographs and a long write up - a wonderful record to keep. Sadly, youthful good news is today not interesting enough.

Girls were looking for something more than the basic programme and more were gaining the coveted Queen's Guide Award and the Duke of Edinburgh Award Scheme was being followed by Rangers.

QUARRIES & CASH

International Camps and Jamborees were becoming more accessible and girls were able to realise the true meaning of a world-wide organisation.

In 1963 Clevedon Guides celebrated their 50th anniversary with a Thanksgiving Service in St. Peter's Church followed by a gathering of ALL members of the movement - 2 Trefoil Guild members were Guides in the first company in Clevedon.

On 6th October 1965 The Hon. Mrs Gervas Clay - daughter of Lord and Lady Baden Powell was the speaker at the Annual General Meeting. Betty Clay, as she is known to all Guides, spoke about the trips she had taken with her mother - the Chief Guide - and how 'a great joy of living comes from Mum'. Surely this must be the best reason for being a Guide.

No change is readily accepted but in September 1967 change came. The volume of members had made this necessary. Clevedon as one District had become too large for one Commissioner to administer. So the challenge was to accept and make the two Districts work. Clevedon East and Clevedon West were born - and survived and grew. Both Districts flourished; there was friendly rivalry - good for standards and morale. New personnel were needed both as Guiders and supporters, new helpers and new blood was a lifeline to both Districts, Guiding continued to grow, although by now there was beginning to be a greater choice for the girl to fill her leisure time.

The Guide Movement - so called because it moves with the times - recognised this trend and continually monitored the needs of the girl and arranged its programme accordingly. Uniform also came under scrutiny and was - and is continually - made more attractive to girls and young women.

1972 was special for many - an International Camp was held by Clevedon Division at the Downs School, Wraxall. Both Districts were very involved with the organisation and staffing of this. Everyone wanted to go, and most did manage a visit but the selection of the few who camped was a difficult task. Lasting friendships were made from many parts of the world and some remain firm today with visits still being exchanged, not only the girls themselves but their respective families have formed a tie through Guiding. The Hon. Mrs Gervais Clay - was present at the closing ceremony; she spoke to all our overseas visitors giving them encouragement to take Guiding into the future, as her parents would have wished.

The Trefoil Guide and the Local association celebrated their 25th anniversaries in 1973. The Swiss Air disaster occurred during this time and the loss of some Guiders from nearby districts affected the whole County.

International visits were now literally 'taking off' and girls and young women were given the opportunity to see how Guides and Girl Scouts followed their programme - sometimes in extremely inhospitable - to our eyes - environments! Guides from the West District went to New York at the invitation of Guides who attended our International Camp in 1972 and a Guide from the East District went to Norway to stay with a Norwegian Guide who had stayed with her family after the camp, the friendship between those two families has lasted up to the present day - all brought about by the meeting of two girls at a camp.

1974 was a year most Guiders in the North of Somerset had been dreading! The new Government Boundary changes brought into being the new County of Avon, stretching further south than the old Bristol County. The Northern area of Somerset became Avon South for Guide Association purposes - Bristol and South Gloucestershire becoming Avon North, and so two new Guide counties were born.

Change, however, brings determination to make it work - and work it did due to the efforts of Guiders in both New Counties. All members were affected if only in the change of county badge or notepaper heading but as with everywhere else Clevedon accepted this change and moved on. Guiding activities continued, Brownies celebrating their Diamond jubilee had special events arranged - special Thinking Day services, and Revels with a 'Diamond' theme. Clevedon Brownies joined the Division for a visit to Bristol Zoo (kindly kept open one evening specially for us) - 700 brown clad girls - no one was lost! but one beret fell into the Monkey enclosure! All members joined the rest of the Division for a Service in Bristol Cathedral. Finally four trees were planted in the Pier Copse on a cold Saturday in November! The year of change ended like any other with each unit Guider searching to provide an interesting and useful purpose for the girls.

During the 1970s Guiding was at its peak in Clevedon, numbers increased, new units were formed and were well staffed. Clevedon East started its money-raising quest for a headquarters - which would take 20 years to come to fruition. These supporters were able to attend the Supporters and Trefoil Guild conference at the Festival Hall in London, returning brim full of new ideas! Clevedon West furthered its links with Canada and the USA, and the Rangers gained high levels working on the Duke of Edinburgh Award Scheme. His Royal Highness visited Clevedon School to see for himself the work carried out by organisations in and around Clevedon, many were privileged to 'shake the royal hand'! Community Service was to the forefront and Guides could be seen locally, providing entertainment, helping with the elderly and looking after children. Those older girls with first aid qualifications helped with St. John's ambulance and Red Cross services.

Overseas visits are now regular occurrences and Guides chosen have unforgettable experiences. The World centres in Sangram (India), Our Cabana (Mexico) and Our Chalet (Switzerland) as well as others in Europe are within sight for the lucky ones. However most girls will remember their camp in Cornwall or the Cotswolds with just as much pleasure.

During this era great pride was taken in the way we looked and presented ourselves to the public, smart uniform and the good conduct of everyone was paramount. Girls wanted to join in and be part of this great movement. Sadly, with the advent of many other activities and amusement this is not so today, perhaps we have quality not quantity in the new century!

QUARRIES & CASH

Jamborees and weekend camps became more popular as Guiders mostly now had full time jobs and their holiday weeks precious for their families. Jamborees have always been popular with the Scout Association and invitation to Guides was welcomed - of course the girls were delighted! Guides from Clevedon enjoyed these weekends at Woodhouse Park, Dryham Park, Credition in Devon and locally at Wraxall. Moots for Rangers and International camps were becoming more popular. Clevedon Guides were keen to attend and high standards were required of these girls.

The 'World Cup' was held instead of Brownie Revels in 1982 courtesy of Clevedon Cricket Club. Two Brownie Fathers who were 'real referees' offered their services and kept order with difficulty. Each pack entered a football team from another country. Roars from the crowd penetrated local homes but fortunately residents came out to watch rather than to complain about the noise 'a few little girls could make'!

Guides made a mosaic of Clevedon Pier which was being restored after having collapsed whilst being tested for safety.

Changes to the Guide Programme occurred during 1984 and this prompted a rush to finish badges and sections already started. Girls trying to gain the Queen's Guide Badge had to pull out all the stops to get finished in time and the first few months of 1984 saw smiling faces in every edition of the local press, proudly holding their badges and certificates. Another move for the Movement and more training for Guiders. Trainings at County Days and at Foxlease - our training centre in the New Forest - were well supported by Clevedon Guiders and Young Leaders, all anxious to provide the Guides and Rangers with the very latest information on the 'New' programme. In none of these changes is our threefold Promise affected, something that sets the Guide Movement apart from other youth organisations:

I promise that I will do my best:
To do my duty to God,
To serve the Queen and help other people,
and
To keep the Guide Law.

Clevedon girls have the extra option for the outdoor activities - the beach. Many 'cookouts' (now known as barbecues) were enjoyed, in all units summer programmes there was always the option of an evening on the beach - weather permitting! Black sacks were always taken for cleaning up operations after summer visitors.

The Trefoil Guild was invaluable for help in units and for badge testing. The two Local Association groups continued with their unstinting support, both District Commissioners reliant on their financial backing for camping equipment, uniforms and help with training expenses. Guiding could no longer be run 'on a shoestring', rent for halls and schools was increasing, badges and uniform more expensive and the new handbooks could not be afforded by every family. With regret weekly subscriptions were increased - some Guiders deploring this wishing to stick with the 'earn what you need' motto. Again we had to move onward with the new times.

1985 saw the Guide movement reach its 75th Birthday, celebrations were held all over the world - including Clevedon! Clevedon's birthday wishes winged across the world to where the sun first rises in New Zealand, carried by a Brownie Guider from the West District to a pack Clevedon Brownies had been corresponding with. Many Clevedon windows shone with candlelight on Thinking Day - the birthdays of Lord and Lady Baden-Powell. Local shops gave us window space for our displays and parties were held to celebrate. Woodspring Parks Department planted a display in our honour on the seafront at the bandstand.

1988 gave us a whole new section RAINBOWS - girls from 5 to 7 years old, dressed in a colour of the rainbow tabard, each group has a different colour. Clevedon soon had two units and then waiting lists! Another first for the movement was the introduction of the new and innovative training scheme for all Commissioners. In this modern era problems and occurrences unthought of in the founder's day are often presented to the Commissioner. Professionals' talks on child and drug abuse are included in training sessions. My involvement as a District Commissioner in Clevedon and then as Division Commissioner gave me experiences to draw on when training new commissioners in the 'management of volunteers'. Clevedon Guiders, unknowingly had much input into this scheme - proof of how well Guiding worked in our Town. Clevedon was the host for the Division to celebrate Olave Baden-Powell's centenary in 1989. 700 gathered on Clevedon Cricket ground for sports and a picnic, finishing with huge campfire. The light disappeared rather earlier than anticipated the fire glowed more brightly and the Brownies eyes got bigger! Avalon '89 - an international camp held at the Kings of Wessex School in Cheddar saw many of us making new friends from far off lands. Clevedon Guides were part of the messenger service at the Royal Bath and West Show (Our County shares this service with Somerset alternately).

1990 a new decade, a new uniform and a new Guiding manual. More change and lots more choice in what to wear - no hats for a start. During the early part of the '90s efforts were made to make life easier for busy Guiders. Paperwork was cut to a minimum the number and length of meetings was reduced. Clevedon East's dream of a Headquarters became a reality on a site at Southey Road, with a local builder and supporter overseeing the work.

1993 was the 50th Birthday of the Trefoil Guild and Clevedon Guild participated fully. Members around the County formed a link-up by handing over a baton to their neighbouring Division using any unusual form of transport, the arrival of Clevedon's Chairman on a child's scooter was an unforgettable sight. Members from Clevedon were present at a moving Region Service in Winchester Cathedral. Contact was made with other Guilds, one in Weymouth and two in South Africa and at home a donation was made to Radio Lollipop at Bristol Children's Hospital. Clevedon East Guide Centre was officially opened on 9th September 1995, after many years of struggle they finally made it! I was honoured to be asked to 'cut the ribbon'!

QUARRIES & CASH

1st April 1996 and we're back in Somerset! Local Government Boundary changes as before! So - change again, new standards, new badges, new everything and more money. A very moving and memorable service in Bath Abbey to dedicate the new Somerset North Standard was held on 30th March and attended by all members of the County, including two coachloads from Clevedon.

The Guide Movement has always been multicultural; drawing its members from all races, creeds and colours. The Promise is central to the programme and was brought 'up to date' changing the wording, but not the meaning, so that all could make it central to their life style.

I promise that I will do my best
To love my God
To serve the Queen and my country
To help other people
And to keep the Guide Law.

Todays girl has many choices for spending her leisure time so its not surprising that membership numbers are down slightly. Clevedon is not alone in having fewer girls to cater for than in the early years. However those units remaining are flourishing and there would be more if Guiders could be found to run them. There are waiting lists for Rainbows and Brownies for the packs that are providing fun and enjoyment still.

As with the Promise the programme for Guides has been updated to suit the young women of the 21st Century. New programme 'Zones' replace the 8 points. These 5 zones will encourage girls to:-

❖ *Lead Healthy Lifestyles by promoting physical, emotional and spiritual well being.*

"Winners of KAHUTEC 1999"
l to r: Caroline Stanton, Fiona Harris, Yvette Williams (Guider), Hannah Robinson, Catherine Soloman (4th Guide Unit)

❖ *Increase awareness of Global issues and of their contribution.*

❖ *Discover new experiences and adventures.*

❖ *Develop self-confidence and self-worth and improve interpersonal and life skills.*

❖ *Promote active citizenship among Guides, developing their awareness of rights and responsibilities for all.*

An exciting programme to be followed at the Guide's own pace, interspersed with games and camping and cookouts and other traditional activities. In the summer of 2000 both East and West Districts buried Time Capsules in the grounds of Clevedon East's Guide Centre, already things have changed! What will the Guides of the future be doing when they unearth our records? They will still have the Promise as central to their programme, but will they be camping in space!

Mary House

Clevedon Amateur Swimming Club

With the development of the sea front in the 1820s, Clevedon visitors and residents were able to take part in the new-found pastime of bathing off the local beaches, when the tide allowed. In addition, Mr. Samuel Taylor built the Marine Baths in 1828/29, on the site now occupied by the bungalow next to the Royal Pier Hotel. The terracing of these old Baths can be seen looking inland from the Pier. These Baths were replaced by Mr. John Vickery in 1876, on the same site. Extra to these facilities, visitors could use the new Hydropathic Hotel, which stood on the site of the Edgarley Court Flats in Wellington Terrace. The Clevedon Mercury advertised the Hotel in 1901:

CLEVEDON HYDROPATHIC ESTABLISHMENT
Fully Licensed as a Residential Hotel
Turkish Baths for Ladies and Gentlemen
Pine, Brine, Sulphur, Needle, Sitz, Douche, Electric bath
Massage and Weir-Mitchell method etc.

At the Local Board of Health meeting on 6th September 1876 a letter was read from Mr. Thomas Lilly complaining that bathers from the new baths were daily climbing over the wall and bathing in the open sea, causing a great loss to him by takings from his bathing machines falling off in consequence.

It was also stated that persons using these baths often indecently exposed themselves to the view and annoyance of people using the pier. The Clerk wrote to the owner (Mr. Vickery) to remedy this by erecting screens.

All these swimming activities developed before the 1914-18 war into the formation of a club called Clevedon Aquatic Sports. They ran regattas mainly off the Pier beach where rafts were moored to use as starting points for 100yd and 70yd races, plank and shovel races and a raft for boxing matches where if one boxer was getting the worst of a bout he could dive off! Local boatmen towed a plank with a surf riding competitor sat astride, and walking the pole was featured on a pole set up off the rocks adjacent to the pier. The Oakhill Brewery (via Mr. Joe Rich?) presented a trophy for men and Mr. & Mrs. Coles of the Pier Hotel a trophy for ladies to be presented to the winners of a swim from Lady Bay to the Pier, this would be the start of the present day "Long Swim".

QUARRIES & CASH

Councillor Frederick Robert Nutting had proposed a marine lake several times but could not get support from his fellow councillors.

Mr. Nutting came originally from the Malvern area and for many years ran a grocers shop at the top of Hill Road where Spilsbury's is now. He believed that a lake would be a great asset to the town so he purchased the foreshore rights with his own money and gave them to the Council. This virtually shamed them into building the lake.

Photograph of Marine Lake and inset Cllr F. R. Nutting

The Contract to build the lake was awarded to J. Moore & Co. of Nailsea, the Engineer was Mr. Gower Pimm of Bristol, his Resident Engineer being Mr. Donald Tyack. The Contract included the provision of a timber club/changing room, a 10m diving board and a spring board.

Building the lake cleaned up a corner of the sea front known locally as 'stinking corner' owing to the debris left from the ebbing tides. A recently restored plaque celebrating Mr. Nutting's achievment is now on view built into the marine lake wall.

On January 15th 1929 a meeting was held at the Royal Pier Hotel of interested parties, and Clevedon Amateur Swimming Club (CASC) was formed. Their brief was to promote swimming, organise galas and take over the long swim from Clevedon Aquatic Sports.

The facilities in place at the lake allowed CASC to apply for affiliation to the Amateur Swimming Association, (ASA), Somerset ASA (SASA) and the Western Counties ASA (WCASA). These affiliations meant that many West of England Championships were held in the

Marine Lake and with prestigious officers such as Sir Charles Miles Bart. and Col. Sidney Keen D.S.O. the Club started off on a firm footing.

The first gala in the lake was held on July 20th 1929, and notable winners were:-

    Mens 100yds - J. Hessel,
    Boys 50yds - A. W. Mead,
    Ladies 50yds - Ms. O. Berry &
    Girls 50yds - Ms. J. Owen.

A water polo team was formed and games on a home and away basis were played against teams from Shepton Mallet, Wells, W-s-M, Bath Admiralty, Bath Dolphins, various Bristol teams and a day trip on the Campbell steamer to play Newport. Before the 1939/45 war the basis of the team was made up from the following:- Alan Porter, Albert Ralph, Mervin & Don Hack, Jack Hessel, Reg Bray, Fred Nichols and Cecil Neads. After the war, other than the players already mentioned a second team was formed consisting of:-
C. Hill, R. Ford, M. Clementson, N. Searle, P. Waterman, D. Genge, A. Fryer, P. Leveret, P. Sandy, F. Chapman and L. Eager.

As some of the opposing teams pools improved it became difficult to arrange home games, also in the early 50s the A.S.A. changed the rules of water polo so that players could now move at all times. This made polo faster and more fatiguing and forced some of the older players into retirement. These changes resulted in a reduction of interest and although an attempt was made to form a team in the mid 60s it was not successful.

After the war the Club resumed under the Presidency of T. T. Miller Esq.,with Chairman Mr. R. J. Hoddell, Treasurer Mr. R. J. Bray and Secretary Mr. G. Gregory.

Galas continued together with club and county championships, and a teaching programme not only for swimming but qualifying for "The Royal Life Saving Association" badges and the "The Amateur Diving Association" diploma. The training reached its peak in the mid 70s when the A.S.A ran a twelve month scheme called "Swimming For All". CASC, although a seasonal club, taught 300 children and adults to swim, coming top of any club in the country!

In an attempt to improve the lake in the early 50s, the Club, with the co-operation of the C.U.D.C. carried out a mud clearing operation at the swimming pool end of the lake. The C.U.D.C. built a wall at the south west corner as a reservoir and an ex-wartime A.F.S. pump with hoses attached to trolleys was manned by club volunteers to wash all the mud from the swimming pool end out through the sluices. The Club also demolished the timber pavilion which had deteriorated over the years, drawings were prepared and the C.U.D.C. built a new pavilion. Club members fitted out the building internally with seating, changing cubicles and decorations and it was then officially opened by Mr. Momber, President in 1953.

The Club continued the "Long Swim" from Lady Bay to the Pier until the early 50s, then to encourage more public involvement the swim was started from the headland of Church Hill to the Pier with ladies starting from the pump house at the Lake. In an attempt to create more interest the swimmers wore numbered polo caps and a commentary was given from the pier to the public over a 'Tannoy' system, but identifying the swimmers was a problem so it had minor success.

Quarries & Cash

The first winners of the "Long Swim" in 1928 were, for the men, Mr. R. E. Strange and, for the ladies Ms. I. Batchelor and many well known Clevedon names followed. In 1953 a Clevedon versus Portishead long swim was introduced, taking place at alternate venues each year, the swim at Portishead was from Battery Point to Sugar Loaf Beach. Each team was made up of four swimmers and the winners were presented with the "Ray Denning Shield". A Junior Long Swim was introduced and Albright and Wilson presented suitably inscribed cups, the first boys winner was Philip Fortune and the girls, Carol Lawrence. Both Philip and Carol went on at a later date to win the senior titles.

H. C. Clementson in the early days of the club was a Somerset diving champion.

George Jarret served as President, Chairman and committee member for 40 years.

A. S. Ralph served 32 years as committee member, Chairman, and Treasurer and played regularly for the water polo team. The club was honoured in 1958 by his appointment as President of the Somerset A.S.A.

R. Bray served 40 years as committee member, Secretary, Treasurer and water polo captain. He represented Somerset at diving, served on the Somerset and Western Counties A.S.A. and was prominent in training young people particularly in diving, bringing several club members up to county and national standards. He was appointed Somerset A.S.A. President in 1971/72.

1950 : Boat for the start of the Long Swim

All clubs require and have people who are stalwarts either in administration or sporting honour for the club. Listed here are a few of many who were members of CASC.

1974 : Rita Gregory being presented with the Ladies Cup by David Bryant

Rita F. Gregory has over a 20 year period served as committee member, Ladies Club Captain, Competition Secretary and has won the Ladies Long Swim 19 times! As well as being ladies club champion at junior and senior levels, she was for 11 years Somerset and Western Counties A.S.A diving champion and represented Somerset nationally. She was appointed secretary to Somerset A.S.A. diving and educational committee.

Steve Price in recent years brought honour to the club by swimming the English Channel, a two way swim from Clevedon to Penarth and back across the Bristol Channel and also a swim across the Irish Sea.

The CASC moved their activities to the new indoor swimming pool built at the Strode Road Centre where galas, training etc. continued, but unfortunately not diving. Many swimmers still use the Marine Lake and some swam all the year round even breaking the ice in winter!

The present club has a strong membership, in fact it has a waiting list of those wishing to join. The Clubs' trophies and entries to the S.A.S.A and W.C.A.S.A. events are still competed for meaning that the Club has continued with the enthusiasm and achievements which have been its backbone since 1929.

Unfortunately Woodspring D.C. and N. Somerset Councils' have removed all the facilities from the Marine Lake and have allowed it, through lack of maintenance, to deteriorate to such an extent that proposals have been made by them to demolish it. This would be a sad day for Clevedon people and visitors who have enjoyed not only swimming but also boating on the Marine Lake.

Laurie Eager

With acknowledgements to Ms. R. F. Gregory, Ms. Jane Lilly, Ms. Curry Smith, Ms. Jenny Ellis, Mr. Mick Clementson, Mr. J. A. Merritt and The Clevedon Mercury.

QUARRIES & CASH

LONG SWIM WINNERS

MENS CUP	LADIES CUP
Presented by Oakhill Brewery	Presented by Mr.& Mrs. B. V. Coles

1928	Robert Strange	1928/31	Irene Batchelor
1929	Cecil Neads	1932/35	Olive Berry
1930/31	Belmont Strange	1936/37	Gwen James
1932	Jack Hessel	1938	Betty Leverett
1933/37	Arthur Berry	1939	Olive Berry
1938/39	Alan Porter		

———————1939/45 War———————

1947/48	Cyril Hill	1947	Jean Flack
1949	Jack Hessel	1948	Joyce Gregory
1950	Mick Sperring	1949	Jean Crane
1951/52, 57, 62	Laurie Eager	1950/67	Rita Gregory
1953/54	Malcolm Hunt	1968/71	Carol Lawrence
1955	Robin Conybeare	1972/73	Norma Lawrence
1956	Frank Chapman	1974	Rita Gregory
1958	Tony Purkiss	1975	Janet Evans
1959/61	Derek Arther	1976/77	Norma Lawrence
1963/64, 67, 79	Len Hurley	1978/82	Alison Ford
1965/66	Bob Fletcher	1983/88	Sarah Smith
1968/72	Philip Fortune	1989/90	Sarah Stone
1973	Bill Barcham	1991/92	Tina Thomas
1974/75, 80	Ken Barcham	1993/94	Hollie Ellis
1976/78	Malcolm Clark	1995/97	Helen George
1981/83	Richard Ball	1998/2000	Charlotte George
1984, 89	Peter Larrad	2001	Charlotte Bullock
1985/86	Steven Smith		
1987/88, 90, 92	Steve Price		
1991	Ross Addicott		
1993/95, 97	Anthony Rowlands		
1996, 98/2000	D. Mitchell		
2001	Luke Whittaker		

JUNIOR LONG SWIM CUPS

Presented by Albright & Wilson

BOYS CUP		GIRLS CUP	
1968/69	Philip Fortune	1968	Carol Lawrence
1970/71	Christopher Ford	1969/71	Norma Lawrence
1972	Paul Backhouse	1972/73	Jill Fortune
1973	Michael Gilmore	1974/75	Janet Evans
1974/76	Donald Brookman	1976	Clare Wainwright
1977, 79	Mark Royce	1977/81	Alison Ford
1978	Richard Ball	1982	Susan Ford
1980	— no entry —	1983/87	Sarah Smith
1981	Alan Walters & Simon Turner	1988	Sarah Stone
1982	Alan Walters	1989/92	Tina Thomas
1983/84, 86	Stuart Crane	1993/94	Hollie Ellis
1985	Ross Addicott	1995	Helen George
1987	—no entry—	1996	Lucy Butt
1988	Ben Pike	1997/99	Charlotte George
1989	James Thomas	2000/01	Charlotte Bullock
1990	Mathew Curson		
1991	Ross Addicott		
1992	James Thomas		
1993/94	Anthony Rowlands		
1995	Oliver Ellis		
1996	N. Carpenter		
1997	John George		
1998	James Russell		
1999	—no winner—		
2000	Jamie Gould		
2001	Luke Whittaker		

QUARRIES & CASH

THE GEORGE JARRET PERPETUAL CUP

For the youngest swimmer to finish the Long Swim course

1978/79	Susan Ford
1980, 82	Louise Kingston
1981	Rebecca Knight
1983	Sarah Smith
1984/85	Ross Addicott
1986	Gregory Williams
1987	Tracey Tulley
1988	James Thomas
1989	Oliver Ellis
1990/92	Hollie Ellis
1993	Emma Neads
1994	Hollie Ellis
1995/96	M. Lambert
1997/99	C. Aldom
2000	E. Copp
2001	Mathew Morgan

LONG SWIM VETERANS CUPS

Introduced in 1994

MEN

1994/99	Len Hurley
2000/01	Andy Smith

LADIES

1994	Jenny Ellis
1995/96	Viv Rowlands
1997/98	Jenny Ellis
1999	Viv Rowlands
2000/01	Jenny Ellis

Clevedon Rifle Club - 1950

The first question one asks, is why was it born and how? The answer is like this. At the end of World War 2, serving personnel in the armed forces, who were eligible for demobilisation, were sent home and back to civilian life. The Home Guard were disbanded and a vacuum created for these people and despite the hardships endured during hostilities for so many, a very strong bond of friendship had been forged during those years and it was felt, that some sort of club or clubs should be created, where those who wanted to, could meet up, have some sort of activity and continue the friendship.

Group photograph taken on the opening night of the Club's new range

In Clevedon, it was suggested that they form a small-bore rifle club, using the existing rifle range at the Territorial Drill Hall on the corner of Albert Road and Hallam Road. From information passed on to me by some of the founder members, this was started under the leadership of Mr. Good as Hon. Secretary, Mr. F. G. Marshall as Hon. Treasurer and Albert Nichols as Club Captain.

The Club joined the re-convened Somerset Small-bore Rifle Association and started to fire weekly "postal matches" with good success, until, a problem was created by the caretaker of the Drill Hall not arriving on the Club Night, to open the premises. This meant, in default of non returned match cards, they were losing matches, which could easily have been won and it was at this time, I came into the picture.

QUARRIES & CASH

Having joined the Territorial Army, (205 Field Company Royal Engineers) in January 1937 (after lying about my age), I very quickly became interested in using the small-bore range in the Drill Hall, under the guidance of Lieut. Lang, who at that time was the second in command. The O.C. was Captain D. L. Rees, the proprietor of a private school for boys in Elton Road. My keenness overtook my other activity of Scouts, from which I resigned and with the help of Lieut. Lang, joined the Tickenham Rifle Club, who fired several teams weekly over the bowling alley at the Tickenham Star. August 1939 came, mobilisation and that was the end of the peace-time sport for me.

In the Royal Engineers, rifle shooting did not figure to any extent in our training, in any case, ammunition was in short supply and we had other more important things to be proficient in, i.e. building bridges, (and blowing them up) in fact anything you can think of, we took it on. One thing we did with great success, was supplying a large hospital in the very south of Italy in 1943, with all the water it needed, the Germans having cut off the normal supply. They certainly used a lot of water and this had to be pumped from wells which were running dry as fast as we could find them.

Peace came eventually and I was demobbed in January 1946, and rejoined J. H. Woodington Ltd., this time, not as the office boy, but as the trainee manager under the guidance of Mr. Tom Roynon. He said to me, "Son, you have 5 years to learn my job" then it is up to you. Thanks to the excellent help and tutoring he gave me, I did take over when he retired and owe him a great deal.

Tickenham Rifle Club was re-started and I once more became a member. Unfortunately for me, it did not seem to have the same feeling as pre-war. Mr. Fred Marshall, who was the Company Secretary at J. H. Woodington, and Hon. Treasurer of the Clevedon Home Guard Rifle Club, invited me to join them and fire in their weekly matches. This I did, but in a very short time, the problem of the non-arriving caretaker on club nights, made me very angry, (I was used to good military discipline) and having burnt my bridges with the Tickenham Rifle Club, by opening my mouth, I found myself on the committee and quickly suggested we build our own Rifle Range! It was at this time, that my wife and I became very strong friends with one of their members and his wife, Ted and Olive Vowles. Ted had been involved in an accident some time previously and as I understood it, was not passed fit for military service, but, this did not deter him from playing a very active role in the Home Guard.

It was very quickly pointed out to me, that there had been a war (as if I did not know) and supplies of all kinds were difficult, if not impossible, to obtain. This word impossible did not figure in the army I knew and where there's a will there's a way. Our secretary took fright, wondering what trouble I was going to create and resigned and I found myself the new secretary.

Now, the task of creating the Clevedon Rifle Club 1950 started.

—ooo000ooo—

The first task was to find a suitable plot of land, where we would not be a nuisance to local people.

My tutor at Woodington's, was not only a retired Captain in the Clevedon Home Guard, but the father-in-law of the Deputy Engineer and Surveyor of the Clevedon Urban District Council, who opened up preliminary investigations, to find out if the Council had any land which would be suitable for our range. Mr. Bill Hand, a "Representative" or "Commercial Traveller" as they were known in those days, whom, as everyone knows, was the leading light in the Clevedon Football Club and also, a Town Councillor, gave a great deal of help. The old saying, "It is not what you know, but, who you know".

Our "contacts" went to work and after some time, the Council offered us a plot of land at West End, Clevedon, "the site of a former quarry, many, many years ago, at a "peppercorn rent" of ONE SHILLING PER YEAR for twenty years. Now it must be recorded here, this was only made possible by the generous help given by Tom Roynon, Bill Hand, Johnny Heywood (Mr. Roynon's son-in-law and Mr. Bill Hurn the Chairman of the Clevedon District Council. Now we had the land, but no plans and no money.

This is where Mr. Johnny Heywood came to the rescue. Contact was made with the National Small-bore Rifle Association and they gave us considerable help regarding safety requirements, etc., etc. In fact a representative came down from London and met Mr. Heywood and myself and told us how to go about the project in hand. A great help.

Plans were drawn up and passed.

While this was going on, wives of members were helping with "jumble sales", they were a good source of income in those days, as consumer durables were still in very short supply. Also, we were selling a type of lottery card, where one tore off a strip to find if you had to pay a small sum, or, receive a small sum. Each card generated a profit of 5 shillings (25p)! Not enough praise can be given to the ladies for their support in finding the money needed when selling these lottery type cards. They would not take no for an answer.

Around Easter 1950, work started and Mr. Heywood joined us at the quarry and with the aid of his surveying equipment, the site was marked out and the real work started. It will be remembered, that previously I have mentioned my very good friend Ted Vowles and it was Ted, who was my constant helper at the site, evenings and Saturdays, when we seldom saw our families.

The first task was to excavate the trench for the foundations. Problem No. 1. we were in a quarry and had to excavate to the required depth, which had to be inspected and passed before laying the concrete. Pick axes were useless, and we finally used sledge hammers and scarifying picks, (those things used at the rear end of the local steam roller when tearing up a road). It was a long and hard task but thanks to the dedicated few, we finally won and the excavation passed inspection.

By this time, enough money had been generated to be able to buy the necessary materials to lay the foundations, all mixed and laid by hand. Again the surveyor came to approve the levels, which had been done with a long builder's plank,

Quarries & Cash

and a 3 foot spirit level and turning the plank and level each plank length, in order to correct any errors. It worked and we were informed we were only half an inch out at one corner!

Now we were faced with the brickwork. First we had to buy the bricks. Again we were lucky, as the Clevedon Brick & Tile Company were exactly opposite Woodington's Boot Factory and it was natural that Mr. Roynon and Mr. Tony May, the Managing Director of the Brick Works and the Clevedon and Portishead Laundry, which was also within a few hundred yards of the Boot Factory, should be good friends and a friendly word on our behalf, enabled the purchase of bricks at a very, very good price, providing we unloaded them from the freshly opened kilns after firing, ourselves. There were not too many volunteers for this task.

We now needed a professional bricklayer. Mr. Fred Marshall, the company secretary at Woodington's, was also well connected with the running of the Clevedon Liberal Club and knew personally, most of its members. One of these was Mr. Jack Garland who lived in Strode Road and was a very professional bricklayer. By gentle pressure Fred Marshall persuaded Mr. Garland to undertake to work for us at 3 pounds 10 shillings per thousand, provided we did the labouring, mixed the mortar to his professional standards and that we would always be on the site, with bricks at the ready, mortar mixed and screeded (no stones or lumps) and he was never kept waiting. We made this promise and worked together, Monday, Tuesday, Wednesday, Thursday evenings, (when it was not raining) and Saturday afternoons for weeks on end, until the brickwork was completed, by which time, we were out of money again. Many times, while the brickwork was going up, I had to get one of the factory ladies to sell another lottery card during the day, in order to purchase a bag of cement in time for the bricklayer that night. We were on a financial knife edge all this time.

It was now around August and holiday time. Timber was required for the roof trusses, but, the problem was, we were once more out of money and no timber licence, which was necessary at that time. One day, Mr Roynon said to me, "what is the matter with the work on the rifle range? I had to tell him, we are out of money, so, have not applied for the timber licence. Well, he said, "Apply for the Licence". I did. It was rejected. I telephoned the Ministry office in Bristol to ask why, only to be told, it was not essential at this time of shortages. I pondered on this for a few days and then decided to write to the War Office and tell them, here were a few volunteers, willing to build and pay for their own range, buy their own ammunition and keep themselves ready for any further outbreak of hostilities and the Ministry of Supply were not prepared to help us, by not allowing us to purchase timber for the roof. About 4 or 5 weeks later, a telephone call to my office from the Ministry at Bristol, informed me that the licence had been granted. However, in the meantime, I heard it was possible to purchase steel trusses which were intended for agricultural buildings. A few discreet telephone calls put me in touch with the Devon Trading Company at Exeter, who told me they could supply me with my needs and gave me a price, including delivery to Clevedon. Very quietly, I told Mr. Roynon about the timber licence and the possibility of the steel trusses, he told me to order the trusses and he would lend me the money for these and timber for the for the roof. This I did, all of which arrived post-haste.

Once again, professional help was at hand. Our Rifle Club Captain, Mr. Arthur Williams, who was the manager of the Co-op in Old Church Road, Clevedon, also lived next door to Mr. Lionel Vaggers, who, was not only a very professional carpenter and joiner, but in former years, had been a site manager for a very large construction company. What could be better? Under his expert guidance, the trusses were erected and well and truly fixed into place. The door was hung and windows fixed. It was at last looking like a building. But again, we were out of money, having directed all our efforts in fund raising, to repaying Mr. Roynon his generous loan. During these difficult times, the ladies' help was magnificent with their money raising efforts, without these, we would never have made it.

History repeated itself. Mr. Roynon, repaid, said to me "when are you going to put the corrugated iron on to the roof?" Again, when we have enough cash to pay for it, which should be in about 4 or 5 weeks. "How much is it" he asked? Devon trading had given me a complete price, (I am not sure now the exact price but it was in the region of £50. Order it now, before winter sets in he replied. No second bidding was necessary. The sheeting arrived, Lionel Vaggers was back again. Roof laid. Bullet catcher constructed, the floor of the range covered with FREE deliveries of ash from Portishead Power Station and we were ready to go, EXCEPT for one thing. The range had to be inspected for safety purposes.

Fortunately, this did not turn out to be a problem and a "Safety Certificate" was duly issued.

Mr. W. Hurn, Chairman of the Urban District Council, examining his result of the very first shot fired on the range

Quarries & Cash

The Clevedon Rifle Club 1950 was opened in November 1950 by Mr. W. Hurn, the Chairman of Clevedon Urban District Council and he had the privilege of firing the very first shot on the range and scored a NINE.

Of course, when we were back on a financial even keel, there was more work to be done, a fire place in the club room, toilet to be built, sewer connected, a trench for the mains water to be connected, the outside of the building rendered, decorating and a few other necessary jobs completed, but they were all done with voluntary labour and all outstanding loans repaid.

This range would never have been built without the very generous financial help given by Mr. Tom Roynon, the help with concession prices from Mr. Tony May, Clevedon Brick & Tile Company, very importantly, the manpower help given by Mr. Jack Garland and his son with the bricklaying and Lionel Vaggers for his very professional skill in erecting and laying the roof.

—oooOOOooo—

Off we went into the Somerset County League, first with one team . . . .

     . . the Mens "A" Team
Later with . . the Mens "B" Team
Later with the . . Mens "C" Team
Later with the . . Ladies Team
Finally with the . . Junior Team
  Boys and Girls of school age.

Carol Potter, a member of the junior team, firing a match target in the Somerset County League watched by her pet labrador, Honey.

CLEVEDON: CLUBS, CAKES,

Mr. Ross Gooby (President) firing a practice target with the pistol section of the club

Finally

The necessary modifications were made to the firing points, to enable us to be approved for .22 (small-bore) pistol shooting, who fired in the English National League and Clevedon had at one time, the only team in Somerset. By our sixth season of Pistol Shooting, our "A" Pistol Team, was rated as 7th in Great Britain. Also, at that time, the "A" Team were firing against teams such as the Special Branch in London. We were also fielding 3 other Pistol Teams, B, C & D and administering the County Pistol Team. During my time with the Club, many of our members fired at Bisley in small-bore and full-bore .303.

After serving the Club for 12 years, I decided the time had come to retire as Hon. Secretary & Treasurer and hand over to a successor who would take them into the future.

One person who has not received a mention and deserves great credit, is Mr. George Ross-Gooby, who for the whole term of my office, was our President. On numerous occasions he gave me some very valuable advice in a quiet and discreet manner.

Mervyn J. Potter

With the success of the pistol teams, a silhouette target set was purchased to give practice for those who attended the Bisley Pistol meetings. At one time, club member Mr. Pat Ifold was selected as reserve shot for the .22 Olympic Pistol Team. However, when the new laws were brought into being regarding the possession of pistols and hand guns, pistol shooting stopped. .22 rifle shooting is still carried on but not in competitive team shoots.

Derek Lilly

QUARRIES & CASH

Clevedon Pier, 1990 - 2001

A resumé of the history and personal reflections by Austin Davis
(with acknowledgements to Angela and Dave Long)

Following my *History of Clevedon Pier [part 2]* which was published in *"Clevedon Past"* in 1993, I now have the pleasure to give the more recent history from 1990 to the present day. I also feel that it is an opportunity to give some personal reflections, as this makes history all the more interesting.

The reopening of the pier on 27 May 1989, was a partial reopening, as only the neck of the pier had been restored. Phase 2 of the restoration remained to be carried out, as the pier head with its buildings and landing stage needed a major replacement and rebuilding programme.

The brief time with Philip Beisley as pier administrator was followed with the appointment of Ivor & Maggie Ashford, as joint piermasters on 19 March 1990. Ivor was also administrator of the pier and secretary to the Pier Trust but preferred the title, piermaster. Maggie instigated the Pier Gallery as one of the leading art galleries in the area. Their partnership saw many initiatives, that within the next decade would see Clevedon Pier develop into a West Country tourist attraction.

The opapi decking, originally bright yellow was turning grey and the pier had just experienced one of the highest tides and strongest winds in living memory. On 26 February 1990 with 7.36am high water and a 13.6 metre predicted tide, driven by a force 12 North Westerly wind, this combination of extreme weather conditions caused much seafront damage. The only damage to the pier was that decking was lifted by the waves hitting the rocks, where the decking meets the incline, this situation was later avoided by making a hinged gate out of the decking, thus giving the waves a chance to escape by lifting the gate. I remember a group of us collecting the length of decking from Lady Bay and returning them back to the pier for reuse.

During 1992 members of the National Piers Society visited the pier and with the help of friends in Clevedon gave an illustrated talk called *"The Primacy of Piers"* at the Community Centre, after which I presented a large collection of pier picture post cards to the Society in memory of my first wife, Margaret Jean Given. This collection has proved a valuable resource and reference collection which may be accessed from the NPS.

The need to show the public that work was still to be carried out was shown by the efforts of a small group of volunteers under the leadership of a retired engineer, Mike Crisp, making use of the skills of various volunteer craftsmen and helpers. The task was to erect one of the shelters, originally on the pierhead to a new position across the width of the incline before the decking starts. The cast iron shelter was in position without its roof covering, as this would have blocked the view of the pierhead. The work was completed by September 1993 and remained in place until 1997. A drawing of this shelter may be found in *"Striding Boldly"* by Nigel Coombes, published in 1995 by Clevedon Pier Trust.

The 125th anniversary of the original opening of the pier was celebrated on Easter Monday 1994, this was followed by a special birthday party on the pier at which a birthday cake, made by my mother of the very best ingredients, was cut by Kayleigh Merchant the granddaughter of Ralph Fryer, the Chairman of the Pier Supporters. This celebration was one of many fund raising and promotional events that were taking place with the aim of keeping the pier in the limelight. I remember the attempted hot air balloon lift off by Don Cameron, the longest skittles alley event organised by the Royal Oak in Copse Road, when at least 200ft of the pier became a skittles alley for the day. I also remember the various times when the pier was used for filming events and the visit by one of HM smaller warships, a minesweeper with a wooden hull.

During 1995 the Pier Trust approached the National Lottery to apply for funding. The National Lottery required strong evidence for such funding and after a lot of paper work, in fact many suitcases full and a visit to London, the grant was acquired in due course. This would allow the pier head, the buildings and the landing stage to be fully restored and see the final completion of the work to the pier.

The work was controlled by English Heritage and saw all sorts of requirements, some of which were almost impossible, for example the use of wrought iron. This had been widely used during the 19th century but could only be found in small quantities from third world countries in the late 20th century. Added to this the insurance company would not sanction its uses. Similar difficulties arose with trying to match the old with what was available to the pier engineers of today.

Mention has already been made of Mike Crisp, who had worked as an engineer in the aerospace industry, but in his retirement restored the cast iron lamp standards and supervised the casting of new ones. These may be found along the length of the pier, with the original examples on the down channel side and replica examples from 1994 on the up channel side. To help pay for the work of fitting these lamp standards, many have been sponsored by individuals, companies and organisations. This example of enterprise had always been a part of the story of seeing Clevedon Pier restored and re-opened to the public.

1995 saw the tragic and fatal road accident in London to Lady Margaret Elton, who had been a trustee up until the early 1980s but had remained as President of Clevedon Pier Supporters until the time of her death. She was very loyal to the those who loved the pier, but like so many

Quarries & Cash

A suggestion for a commemorative plate for the Re-opening of Clevedon Pier, 23 May 1998

© 11. 11.97 Austin Davis

others who had worked hard, did not live to see the pier fully restored and reopened in its entirety. The names of many supporters are to be seen on a plaque in the Toll House.

The Pier Supporters had been formed in 1971 and became a registered charity in 1983. This small group of friends had raised something in the order of £25,000 during its 27 years as a charity and supported the pier with fund-raising and promotional events. The charity celebrated its 25th anniversary in July 1996 with an event at Triangle Farm, home of Mr & Cllr. Mrs Norman Baker. The event was memorable with a marquee and a band. Julia Elton officiated, standing in for her brother Sir Charles, who had accepted the presidency of the supporters. The founder members of the supporters present were Jo and Mike Hedger, Cllr Hilda Baker, Cmdr Tom Foden, Don Metcalf, Nigel Coombes and myself. The charity disbanded as a group in November 1998, as this complied with law and the feeling that the task was complete. At the time Ralph Fryer was Chairman and Hilary Tinkling was Vice Chairman. The Tinkling family have a long association with the pier, (Hilary's father-in-law), the late Wilf Tinkling had a grandfather, who as a young man worked on the original building and is photographed doing so in 1868.

At this time, with the news that lottery funding was available plans were being prepared for Phase 2 to commence. One of the plans of action was to try to put together peoples' memories of what the pier head buildings had looked like when they were in place. Very few photographs had been taken, the most useful strangely enough had been those taken after the pier head had been isolated for about twelve years. It must be remembered that from 1970 - 1982 no one had stepped onto the pier head, the buildings and the decking had formed the home for thousands of starlings. This lack of visual material should remind us that it is important to record photographically buildings and structures as a means of putting things back as they were originally, if the need ever arises.

The layout of the buildings as first erected in 1894 was all a part of the requirement of seeing the Victorian architecture back in place. The caravan shaped, wooden dance hall erected during the 1920s was not being replaced, as it was not the original plan. The engineering work on the pier head commenced in 1997, with the Mowlem Group as main contractor. Hyder Consulting were the consulting engineers and Peter Ware was appointed architect. The work did not progress as rapidly as one would have liked, the very nature of restoration is difficult and slow, especially so in a marine environment. But all credit should be given to the men who used their skills in so many ways, the divers for example who worked in muddy cold water on replacing concrete to the landing stage. It was the divers who unearthed the original 1869 greenheart piles of the first pier head. Again enterprise was seen as the greenheart was used to make small objects for the souvenir shop and on a larger scale with the sculpture erected in memory of Peter Ware, the architect who died just prior to the pier being given a Civic Trust award. This is seen just outside of the Toll House.

QUARRIES & CASH

The Pier Supporters had the great privilege of sponsoring the weather vane, that sits on top of the pavilion at the pier head, this was priced at £1,500 but the supporters were pleased to hand over £2,000 to Niall Phillips, the Chairman to the Pier Trust. Such iron work should be studied in detail as it comprises of very fine artistic casting. The illustration (p. 39) the only detailed one in existence was taken from the actual item whilst it was being restored in workshops in Bristol. Sadly the original plans were non existent as with much of the work of Victorian engineers and architects, their working drawings were not kept for future generations.

In September 1997 the Pier Trust formed a committee with the object of organising an official reopening day, the date was set for Saturday 23 May 1998. The meetings were held first of all every two weeks but as time progressed, there was a meeting every week. Cllr. Richard Hickling chaired the meetings. The time and effort paid off with a most magnificent day with the Royal Marines Band, displays in the air and on the water, with all manner of events on the seafront and in the town. As with the original Victorian opening to the pier there was a procession, many of us dressing as Victorians. School children, councillors, pier supporters and the uniformed organisations marched to the Royal Marine Band. The final event was a firework display, the most outstanding in living memory. An estimated 30,000 people took part in the celebrations and a considerable profit was made for the good of the pier. Sir Charles Elton Bt. and David Bryant CBE of bowling fame officiated, the fifth time that the pier had been opened or reopened, the other dates following the original 1869 event, being 1893, (new pier head), 1913, (landing stage) and 1989 (the neck).

I remember the 7am start to the day, as I was erecting a stall on the seafront at that time in readiness for a day of blowing up and tying hundreds of balloons, and launching them off from the pier head. These gas filled balloons all flew south some of which reached northern France, a previous event saw balloons going east with several reaching Poland.

Clevedon Pier was voted, "Pier of the Year" in 1999 and I travelled to Paignton with a group from Clevedon to receive the award from the National Piers Society. 1999 was also important in other ways but from a more personal point of view, I proposed to my second wife, Mary Elizabeth Bertram during April, there being a seat with a brass plaque in one of the shelters to commemorate this occasion, paid for by our pier friends. We later had some of our wedding photographs taken on the pier head. Many couples these days are finding the pier a romantic place for their engagements and in time weddings may be conducted or blessed on the pier.

A mention of the brass name plaques must be made at this point as they form a very important revenue for the pier, but perhaps more importantly they give everyone the opportunity of having their name 'stamped' on the pier. In time one could say that these plaques will form a valuable resource for social historians. Visitors may be seen at all times looking for their name plaques, up and down the decking.

The start of the year 2000 saw the death of Ivor Ashford, a true gentleman and joint piermaster since 1990 along with his wife, Maggie. He was very much respected and his loss was deeply felt in the town. Today Maggie is joined by her daughter, Lucy, along with the continuing support of volunteer helpers and friends.

Later in the year the death of Bernard Faraway, who was Piermaster from 1949 until 1970 was reported upon in the *"Mercury"*. He loved the pier and lived in the Toll House for many years with this wife, Joan and son, Geoffrey. Bernard always kept an interest in the campaign, the restoration and the day to day life of the pier. The pier, during his time in office, was owned by the local council and when the pier collapsed in 1970 Bernard was seen struggling through the tide saving what he could with the help of Roy Lovelock in the motorboat "Elizabeth" owned by Mervyn Fry. The "Elizabeth" was one of two motor boats, which took the public around the bay.

Mention must be made of the Pier Trust who administer the running of the pier and who hold the 99 year lease from the local District Council. The Trust under the Chairmanship of Niall Phillips are responsible for the future financial credibility and structural maintenance of this Grade 1* listed building. The Trust has also in more recent years taken over the running of Clevedon Heritage Centre, so the full title of the trust is "Clevedon Pier and Heritage Trust". The safety of the public is of vital concern and by 1995 half a million had visited the pier, the one million mark should have been reached by the year 2000. Many of these would have been passengers for the "Waverley", "Balmoral" and "Oldenburg", the pierhead being in full use, even when it was not rebuilt or restored. Temporary measures provided a safe access onto the landing stage during the years when only the neck had been re-opened. It is estimated that the annual maintenance costs to the pier will be around £25,000 at least for the next 50 years. The pier must never be allowed to fall in need of repair. I am confident that with professional engineering care, the structure should stand the test of time. We will no longer accept weight tests for insurance purposes without inspecting the basics of the structure, as was the case between 1952 and 1970.

The total restoration costs amount to; £3.5m, phase 2 costing over £750,000 made up of the National Lottery grant of £475,000 and £250,000 from North Somerset District Council. The gates to the pier were the £20,000 gift of American, Bill Colson, owner of the Hawthorns retirement residence on the seafront.

The year 2001 saw the first meeting of Clevedon Pier Friends with the view of setting up a group of interested people with a youth section called the "mudlarks". Maggie Ashford the piermaster since the death of her husband, Ivor during January 2000, retired in October. The appointment of a new piermaster, was made after national advertising and 100 applicants.

Clevedon Pier has in so many ways been the centre of our lives for around thirty years. Personally my time has been served, I was a founder member of the Supporters. In 1979-1980 I joined the campaign committee which helped to save the pier; from October 1980 - 1998 I served as Honorary Secretary to the Supporters and from 1997-98 I formed part of the organising committee for the official 1998 reopening day. I have had the opportunity of knowing and meeting many like-minded people from all walks of life, this has been interesting and of real value in so many ways.

I give talks on behalf of the Pier Trust and took a large party from the Victorian Society on to the pier during the summer of 2000. They were fully appreciative of the architectural and engineering elegance of the structure and its historical significance. Clevedon Pier today stands not only as a Victorian masterpiece but as an example of 20th century enterprise, with its more recent history. Clevedon should be proud in having such an important structure as part of its townscape. It serves a purpose in so many ways, in our recreational and social well being. I say love it, look after it and above all use it.

Austin Davis

The Weather Vane - Clevedon Pier
Erected 1894 (Engineer - G N Abernethy)
Restored 1997 (Mozier & Co. Bristol)
for Clevedon Pier Trust Ltd.
Sponsored by Clevedon Pier Supporters

Further references

History of Clevedon Pier [part 1]
    [part 2]
'Striding Boldly'
The Grand Reopening of Clevedon Pier
The Guide to British Piers, 3rd Ed.
National Piers Society - Website

Elton, MA. 'From the Village to the Town', CCS 1981
Davis, A. 'Clevedon Past', CCS 1993
Coombes, N. Clevedon Pier Trust 1995
Souvenir Programme 23 May 1998
Mickleburgh,T.J. National Piers Society 1998
www.piers.co.uk

Clevedon Performing Arts Clubs

Beginners Please - Act 1

A personal history of the Clevedon Light Opera Club

May 1952, nearly 23 years old, between girl friends and at a loose end when I went to see a performance of The Gondoliers at the Salthouse Pavilion. A note in the programme invited anyone interested in joining the Clevedon Light Opera Club to contact the secretary.

I had recognised quite a few people I knew taking part in the performance on stage and in the orchestra and they were obviously enjoying themselves so I contacted the secretary and was invited to attend a rehearsal to take an audition. (After 50 years I am still waiting for official confirmation of the result!)

I attended the next week's rehearsal for 'The Mikado' and wasn't shown the door so I presumed I was 'in'.

There had been some division in the Committee on the choice of show for May 1953, Coronation Year, 'Merrie England' or 'The Mikado'. The latter won to the dismay of some stalwart members who were so incensed that they left the club. This was quite a blow as CLOC could ill afford to loose valuable talent but the Club survived the crisis to put on the chosen show. Patriotism showed through however as Pish-Tush wore a miniature Union Jack in his wig! All the male chorus were instructed to 'get their hair cut' so that wigs could be worn properly.

The Club at this time was three years old and had, in the summer of 1949, started virtually on the pavement outside Six Ways Post Office when three members of Clevedon Choral Society met by chance and mentioned that some members would like to present more secular music. A meeting was called resulting in the formation of the Clevedon Light Opera Club and in no time at all 'Merrie England' was rehearsed and presented.

In 1950 a double bill of 'Merrie England' and 'Trial by Jury' showed a profit of twelve shillings and sixpence (62.5p) and the Club was on its way. 1951 saw 'Iolanthe' produced and in 1952 'The Gondoliers' as I mentioned above.

Rehearsals took place wherever suitable space could be found; the Coachhouse in Highdale Road; the Blue Room at Christ Church; the old British School in Chapel Hill (later Bumble Market and now a modern housing development); The Little Harp Inn; an upstairs room at The Waggon & Horses; the Main Hall of Highdale School and the Hall at the rear of the Conservative Club. Our excellent pianist-accompanist was the lady who also played the viola in the Clevedon Light Orchestra for our productions.

The Salthouse Pavilion where our productions were staged had its limitations - only about 9 feet headroom and virtually no wings, minimal lighting equipment and two boxes at the back of the stage contained the toilets—Elsans! The dressing rooms we could just about cope with, two small rooms off the main hall for the ladies and a fifteen foot marquee erected at the rear with a canvas awning to the stage door for the men.

After each performance all costumes, make-up, equipment, props and bar stock had to be removed to the stage for safety and judiciously placed to miss any leaks from the roof.

During those early years we hired scenery but it was always too big for the stage and the carpenter's saw was in great demand. As a result we started to construct our own scenery, a tradition which has continued to the present day. Costumes were always hired from one or other of the national costumiers, and what a tale can be told of ill fitting uniforms and dresses - panic stations for the wardrobe mistress as they did not normally arrive until about the Friday before the show, but by opening night they had usually been 'doctored' and fitted fairly well.

The Salthouse Pavilion was a popular centre in Clevedon until it was demolished in 1962 and replaced by a block of flats. It was used for dances, concerts, displays and so on and being totally enclosed could be used at any time of the year without the intrusion of daylight. The move to the New Hall at Sunhill Park restricted performances to darker nights and March became our regular production date.

'The Mikado' in 1953 was followed in '54 by 'The Rebel Maid' then in the next two years 'Pirates' and 'The Yeomen of the Guard' this being our last G & S production.

Two memories I have of the 'Pirates' were when, during an enthusiastic waving of the flag, the knob of the Jolly Roger flagpole flew off into the audience, and then later the Sergeant of Police marching back and forth on the stage totally unaware that his flies were undone despite giggles from the audience.

Much water has passed under the bridge since those days in 1953. Many shows have been presented and thousands of patrons have "deafened our ears with applause".

Copious notes have been written concerning CLOC's activities in the second half of the last century and hopefully these will be collated into a much fuller account of the life of the Club at some time in the future.

Gordon Lawrence
Life Member, Clevedon Light Opera Club.

A History of "The Clevedon Players" from its inception in 1962

In 1962 two Clevedon amateur dramatic clubs "The Clevedon Playgoers Club" and the "Coleridge Players" amalgamated to form "The Clevedon Players" and there began a society that has spanned nearly four decades. At that time the Playgoers had performed at the St. John's Hall and the Coleridge Players at the long since defunct Salthouse Pavilion.

The first play as the newly formed Clevedon Players was 'Watch it Sailor' by Philip King and Falkland Cary, an every day story of the Hornett family, and there among the cast list is Kathleen Cridland as Edie Hornett. Kathleen is today (2000) still going strong as Secretary to the committee of the club, truly a founder member. During that season the membership fee was 12/- (60p) and this princely sum entitled you to see all four plays produced that season.

1963/64 was the Season of Comedy and included 'The Irregular Verb to Love' with Kathleen Cridland and another stalwart founder member Eileen Ganniclifft. The lighting crew included another original member, Michael Clark and the play was produced by Victor Smith. The membership of the club during that season stood at 475 and by the last play of the season the next four plays had already been chosen, all to be presented on the stage of the Clevedon Community Centre, New Hall marking the start of the association between the two organisations. A jumble sale during that year raised £20. As the years went by many plays of great variety were produced and the following are some of the highlights.

1964/65/66 -'Hobsons Choice','A Touch of the Sun' produced by Peter Ganniclifft and featuring Bill Boddy and Gerry Parker. 'This Happy Breed' featured Laura Smith, ex-Vice President and 99 years old in 2000, together with Doug Stinchcombe. Assistant Stage Managers were Trevor Cridland and Morley Hack who still fixes the ladies' hair as well as 'doing' wardrobe.

1966/67 - Notably 'Goodnight Mrs Puffin' with Kath Cridland as Mrs Puffin and, with the backstage crew, Michael Bright handling lighting. Front of House management was handled by Ray Freeman.

1968/69 A milestone year when 'The Rattle of a Simple Man', produced by Phillip Morris, won the Bristol Evening Post Rose Bowl Dramatic Award. This resulted in performances at the Bristol Theatre Royal with a cast including Anita Conn, Frances Ford and Gerry Parker.

Over the next few years we had 'The Killing of Sister George', 'All Things Bright and Beautiful', 'Wait Until Dark' directed by Muriel Stephens and a cast including Phillip Morris, John Phillips, Maureen Telling and Barbara Stinchcombe.

QUARRIES & CASH

1971 was memorable for 'I Remember Mama' with over 50 people being involved in the production, where did they all come from! The large backstage crew was managed by Peter Morgan and Alan Smith with Maureen Smith helping with properties. 'Victoria Regina' in 1972 had Julie Hawkings playing Victoria and again, a large cast and backstage crew, many of whom are still members today.

The 1974/75 season saw a number of significant events, the formation of "The New Image", a group of predominantly young people who presented 'An Evening Bits and Pieces', then Peter Ganniclifft's production of 'An Inspector Calls' won the Butlins Best Production Award. This was followed up by 'There's a Girl in My Soup', produced by Phillip Morris and judged runner up for the Evening Post Rose Bowl Competition. Maureen Smith won the Bristol Drama Festival Best Actress Award for her part in that play. Also in that season 'The Prime of Miss Jean Brodie' was produced by Barbara Graham another member who has been frequently involved in both acting and directing.

The next few seasons saw 'Crown Matrimonial' a lavish production directed by Muriel Stephens with a cast including Joan Osborne, Jo Cooper, Joyce Smith (a regal Queen Mary) John Riley and Francis Ford. The junior group wrote and produced 'Bear and his Magic Basket' and after a scorching summer the Players put on 'Barefoot in the Park'. The rains that followed caused flooding in "The Stables" at the rear of the Community Centre, an accommodation which was used for meetings and storage, but in wet weather folks still gathered for songs, jokes, storytelling and folk music from John Cowley.

More successes in various competitions were notched up as the seasons went by and more names came to the fore, Anne Legget, Michael Luker, Corrie Goss and Patrick & Joyce Lockstone.

After producing some 17 plays, Muriel Stephens produced George Bernard Shaw's 'Arms and the Man' as her final effort before 'retiring' from this activity but she continued to keep a friendly eye on things for some time.

The 1980's saw a great diversity of productions with some extreme contrasts - 'Confusions', 'Shakespearian Fantasia' a collection of excerpts from the "Master's" Plays, then 'I am a Camera', 'Anastasia' with many regulars in the cast including Alan Cooper as the Sleigh Driver, his second appearance for the Players and still going strong! 'Abigails Party' was followed by 'Life With Father' with Nigel Aylett and Julie Hawkings as Father and Mother.

Entry into the HTV Festival of Drama One Act Play competition with 'The Bespoke Overcoat' directed by Joyce Collins didn't win the competition but Michael Garrick won the Best Actor Award for his part of 'Fender'.

Extending themselves yet again Maureen Smith directed the Players in 'Oh What a Lovely War' with a cast of 24 on stage and 20 backstage and front of house. Another contrast,'She Stoops to Conquer' was directed by Anne Leggett after a four year break.

So the decade went on with productions including 'Witness for the Prosecution', 'Outside Edge', 'Trap for a Lonely Man', 'The Matchmaker', 'Something's Afoot', and 'Under Milk Wood' This latter was a Barbara Graham production in the round with the cast of 41 including quite a few young people from our thriving youth group, Polly Garters baby being real live 6 months old, Bethany Lunam. Now 15 years old, Bethany is following grandfather Alan Cooper's activities on the amateur stage. The young people were ably led by Carole Hockedy who had earlier made a directorial debut when she entered the 1983 HTV Drama Festival by presenting the one act 'When the Bough Breaks' at 3 venues receiving very good adjudications. Our Silver Jubilee Season 1987/88 included 'When we are Married' produced by Peter Ganniclifft and the decade ended with 'Seasons Greetings', & 'A Chorus of Disapproval' both produced by Maureen Smith, 'The Secret Diary of Adrian Mole' & 'Daisy Pulls it Off' produced by Felicity Peries, 'Noises Off' and 'Major Barbara' directed respectively by Carole Hockedy and Judith Robinson.

A disastrous fire in 1990 which rendered the Stables unusable caused the loss of many props, flats and furniture; together with smoke and water damage to our entire wardrobe. A whole army of members and friends moved in while the ruins were still smouldering to salvage everything that was not actually ashes and sterling work by Brookes Dry Cleaners and others restored a large part of our wardrobe. Mrs Bush of Kingston Seymour offered to store our wardrobe, Dr. McLeod stored the props, and the flats and scenery, rebuilt by members, were stored at a local factory through the good offices of John Burns. All this super effort allowed us to continue our productions with some semblance of normality.

An all female cast in the controversial 'Bazaar and Rummage' was directed by Jean Harding. In spite of the language the play was well received and other notable productions followed with 'Cider With Rosie', & 'What the Butler Saw' just to show that the 'Players' were always ready to rise to a challenge. Probably our best ever box office success was Carole Hockedy's direction in April 1992 of 'Allo Allo', compiled from the popular TV series.

The seasons went on showing that the 'Players' could mount almost anything they wished—'Educating Rita' followed by 'Good Companions' then into 'Taking Steps' with many of the female members learning to tap dance and 'Blood Brothers' directed by Maureen Smith. Her next production 'Run for your Wife' included a real life drama when Alan Cooper playing the part of Detective Sergeant Porterhouse and struggling with angina was rushed into hospital at 5.30am on the Sunday morning after the final performance and end of show party on the Saturday evening.

More excellent productions followed - 'Out of Order' directed by David Kenworthy and then a collaboration with The Comedy Club to present 'When the Lights Come on Again' written by Val Vella from W. J. Richard's diary and directed by Carole Hockedy. The piece was presented to commemorate the 50th anniversary of the end of the Second World War and featured a cast of over 70 members of both clubs. Both clubs were able to bring back the props, flats and wardrobe from the various places they had been stored for the last 4 years.

Quarries & Cash

1995/96 had critical and audience success for 'Servant of Two Masters' and 'Salad Days' but equally engaging 'Dancing at Lughnasa' drew the lowest audience figures for some time. 'Rebecca', 'A Christmas Carol' and 'It Runs in the Family' were directed by Gerry Parker, Val Vella and David Kenworthy and during the rehearsals of the latter play the lead player had to withdraw, his place being taken by David giving a 'bravura' performance with very little rehearsal and using the book. Shortly after this he moved from his position of Assistant Chief Constable of Avon & Somerset to Chief Constable in Yorkshire. 'The Darling Buds of May' directed by Judith Robinson received excellent crits in the Rose Bowl competition with Bob Beale as 'Pop Larkin' nominated for Best Actor and Julie Hawkings as 'Miss Pilchester' nominated for Best Supporting Actress which indeed she went on to win!

The 1998/99 season saw Rosmarie Simmonds making her directorial debut with 'Rumours' by Neil Simon followed by `Maria Marten or Murder in the Red Barn' directed by Felicity Peries using the oldest available script for this ancient melodrama. The audience was invited to hiss the Villain and cheer the Righteous. Once again Felicity was able to bring together a `cast of thousands' and everyone seemed to enjoy themselves `With jolly old English cheer and plenty of Beer'. The 'Cemetery Club' was an evocative and moving piece directed by Jean Harding and then our next choice 'Les Liasons Dangereuses' had to be set aside owing to casting difficulties and was replaced by 'The Dresser' directed by Carole Hockedy. We had difficulties in the next season when, after 'Funny Money' and 'The Witches' we had to replace 'Les Liasons' a second time because of the refusal of a licence by Samuel French owing to a professional performance being put on in Bath within 14 days of our proposed production. Anyway at quite short notice we fielded 'An Evening of Alan Bennett' doing 'Bed among the Lentils', and 'Lady of Letters' with Rosie Simmonds and Jean Dolphin respectively giving us a 'tour de force' in these parts, however did they learn it all? The evening was rounded off with 'An Englishman Abroad'.

A history of the Clevedon Players would not be complete without paying tribute to some of those people who through the years have run the 'backstage' of our productions, the list of course is endless, but to mention a few we had Patricia & David Clark, Irene Wessel, Mary Cridland, Paul Wright, Hugh Clark, Joan Stephens and Peter Hurrell all busy during the 60s. Then Derek Wright, Keith Jemison, Vivienne Norris, Alan Smith, Peter Morgan, Mildred Tivney and Heather Dodd during the 70s. The 80s and 90s have been served by Ian Fisher, George & Jayne Taylor, John Burns, Mike Duggan, Tim Bibbings and Chris Cooper. Finally, not to forget our Front of House, Ray Freeman who was always there in the early days through to Bill Dawe in the later days. So here ends this stage of the history and we wonder what the next 40 years in our continuing story will bring.

Alan Cooper
May 2000

Clevedon Comedy Club

Clevedon Comedy Club is now celebrating its 30th year. It was formed when a few people (Maureen & Alan Smith, Doug & Barbara Stinchcombe, Sid Martin and Frank Chesterman) were rehearsing for an entertainment at a Harvest Supper. After rehearsal all went back to the Smith's for coffee and discussed the type of show that was missing in Clevedon. That was on 20th September 1970. There was already in existence a Drama Club and an Opera Club, but at that time nothing in light entertainment - and nothing to encourage youngsters to join. It was decided to aim for a family club and concentrate on light entertainment and pantomime. It would be called The Comedy Club.

The group formed a committee and the first meeting was held on 27th September and the rules made. In October that year, Tom O'Sullivan the Mercury Drama Critic was advised, and after a write-up by him, the inaugural meeting was held at Sunhill in November, Bunny Ayres being asked if he would be the first President. The first production, a variety show "The Roaring 20s" started rehearsal in January of the following year, 1971. The show was produced by Jack Hawdon, compiled by Doug Stinchcombe, MD was Winifred Ayres with Sid Martin as Choreographer and Alan Smith as Stage Manager and it was performed in June of that year.

The first write-up by Tom O'Sullivan stated "Roaring Twenties a Roaring Success" - a club has been born. This then encouraged more people to join and the first pantomime, "Aladdin" followed in January 1972. The Club has produced a pantomime every year since - winning the coveted Rose Bowl twice, with "Puss in Boots" produced by Doug Stinchcombe in 1981 and with "Little Miss Muffet" produced by Val Vella in 1995.

Most years a revue type show is also produced. The Club has only deviated once - when they put on a musical play produced by Victor Smith in October 1975 - "Brothers Ruin" which was also a success.

Apart from stage shows, the Club has done a lot of Charity Shows at Farleigh Hospital; Leigh Court; Ham Green; Yatton Hall and various homes for the elderly.

In this 30th year "Cinderella" was produced in January, assembling the largest cast seen on stage for many years, and this augers well for the future. Roger Lovell, who has held the office of Chairman for the past 20 years has now stood down and he becomes our new President. Founder members Maureen and Alan Smith, are still members and strong supporters of the Club.

On Saturday 22nd September 2001, The Clevedon Comedy Club celebrated the end of their 30th Anniversary year with a Dinner and Disco at the Crabtree Park Hall. It was quite a task to try to trace and contact as many past members as possible as so many had got married, moved away, or sadly passed away. However a good response was received from past members who we did manage to contact, and we were delighted to have founder members Maureen and Alan Smith and Evelyn Martin with us. Past members travelled from as far afield as the Midlands and Cheshire to take part in the celebrations and a great evening was had by all. Many of our newer members had seen videos of past shows and recognised some of the past members! A photo display and past programmes were onshow, and we are now looking forward to 10 more successful years before we celebrate our 40th Anniversary!

Val Vella
2001

The Comedy Club Cast on Stage in 1979 for the "RETURN TO THE FORTIES"

Clevedon Gilbert & Sullivan Society
A Brief History

In 1972 a group of teachers at Clevedon Comprehensive School (now Clevedon Community School), together with parents and with the support of members of some church choirs in the Town, decided to put on a performance of 'Trial by Jury' as an end of term event to raise money for the School Association. It was an outstanding success and it was from these humble beginnings that the Clevedon School Association Gilbert & Sullivan Society was born. The following year saw a performance of a full-length opera, 'H.M.S. Pinafore'. The motivator, Ron Tripp, a teacher at the School, also re-formed the Town Band and the Choral Society.

Between 40 and 50 people took part in the shows at the School in the early years accompanied by an orchestra of about 20. By 1994 these numbers had only dropped very slightly to about 40. It is difficult to imagine now how we managed to accommodate so many on what is a relatively small stage.

The Society continued to put on annual performances at the School until 1994 when members decided that it was time to break the links with the School and move the performances to the Princes Theatre at the Community Centre.

Pirates of Penzance - 1976
Frederick . . . . Vernon Weids,   Ruth . . . . . Doreen Williams

QUARRIES & CASH

(The Society had already changed its rehearsal venue to St. Peter's Hall in Alexandra Road by this time and it had become noticeable that there was less support for the Society both from within the School and within the School Association which prompted the move. Also there were better facilities at the Community Centre, the Gym and Gym changing rooms at the School could be bitterly cold in February).

During the period at the School, the Society had made gifts to the Arts Faculty in lieu of charges and had helped to maintain stage assets such as scenery and lighting.

The Society has successfully competed in local Gilbert & Sullivan competitions, has received nominations for the Rose Bowl awards and, in that competition in 1989, our leading lady won 'The Most Outstanding Musical Performer Award' for her performance in 'Ruddigore'.

The Society changed its name when it cut its links with the School to Clevedon Gilbert & Sullivan Society.

The first performance at the Prince's Theatre in February 1995 was 'Iolanthe'.

The last years at the School and the first couple at the Prince's Theatre proved to be financially difficult for the Society but, due to prudent budgeting and control, the Society is again on a firm footing. Coupled with this has been a growth in the audiences who are, no doubt, enjoying the innovative productions which still remain true to the music of Sullivan and the lyrics of Gilbert. The inclusion of additional dialogue relating to current or local issues and to recent events, in true Gilbertian style, has added interest to the productions.

For example, we have used a small tracked JCB digger in 'The Mikado' in 1998 and Teletubbies lookalikes and a talking head in Ruddigore in 1999. Our 2000 production of 'Pinafore' was done with 'Trial by Jury' becoming an Act 3 Court Martial with an Italian jilted bride, Italian bridesmaids and a Counsel called Pavagrotti. In 'The Sorcerer' in 2001 there were take offs of 'Who wants to be a Millionaire' and 'The Weakest Link' as well as a magic show with a little Pokemon.

The Society's current membership of 45, whose ages range from 6 to 80, still contains a number of members who have been with it from the initial production and who still take an active role in the shows.

There has been a relatively small number of Musical Directors over the years, 9 in total and a slightly larger number of Producers, 12.

The Society has always been pleased to put on concerts during the Summer months for the benefit of charities and for fund raising events. In November 2000 it held its first Gala Night, including a performance of 'The Zoo' at the Prince's Theatre which proved to be a big success.

It has been the Society's aim to support activities in the Town. This we normally do in appropriate costume of the Gilbert & Sullivan era. We were proud to be invited to sing at the end of the Pier as the crowd came down to board The Waverley paddle steamer at the grand re-opening on 23 May 1998 and, on the same day, support the traders in Hill Road with a concert in the afternoon. On this occasion we managed to pull such a large audience that they spilled into the road and it remained closed until the police eventually arrived to clear it. The Society also performed on the seafront at the unveiling of the Millennium Plaque.

In 2002, the Society's 30th anniversary performance will be 'The Gondoliers'.

Roger Carroll
Chairman. May 2001

The Sorcerer - 2001
Clockwise from top left:
Emma Soloman, Danann McAleer, Jane Carroll
Nichola Carroll, Becky Carroll, Samantha Brown.

❈ ❈ ❈ ❈ ❈ ❈ ❈

QUARRIES & CASH

About 100 years ago two young lads, brothers, in Lydney were looking for something to do to provide some pocket money and found that the local baker Mr. William Weaver wanted a couple of errand boys. So Frank Hale and his elder brother George were soon to be found, as early as 5.30 am on some days, delivering bread and cakes to the boats waiting for the tide in Lydney docks and to customers around the town before going off to school.

Good Friday morning was taken up with delivering baskets full of hot Hot Cross Buns to people who had placed their orders earlier in the week.

On leaving school Frank got a full time job in Mr. Weaver's bakehouse and then he was called up for service in the 1914-18 war in the Royal Army Service Corps mainly on overseas duties.

During one of his leaves he met Daisy Andow and at the end of the war when Frank left the Army they were married. He put his early work experience to good effect by opening a small bakery business in Staple Hill, Bristol. One day, Daisy made a sultana cake which so impressed Frank that he thought it might have a much wider appeal. Daisy's recipe was scaled up to bakery sized proportions and they went into production of a cake which eventually became famous throughout the West Country as Hale's Farmhouse Cake.

They soon needed room for expansion and in 1928 moved to East Clevedon where they took over Mr. Parson's double fronted shop and bakehouse at 169 Old Street and concentrated on cake making.

In 1929 his equipment consisted of a small oven and a growing number of staff. Some of the first to join the Company were Walter Reed and Ivor Weids who both stayed on for 50 years. On his first morning, Walter was told to put mince pies on a tray for the shop and proceeded to place them carefully, one at a time. "What do you think the good Lord gave you TWO hands for?" roared the boss - "Get a move on!" Work Study had a long pedigree at Hale's!

CLEVEDON: CLUBS, CAKES,

Mr & Mrs Hale

'Pop' Rose
Cake Decoration expert

Mr Hutchings
Chief 'Sponger'

Van sales team
left to right: Les Rendel, Ted Clothier, Ron Small (vanboy), Mervin Carey,
Bill Searle, Ray Feest and Len Haskins

Van No. 41 - The Show Van

QUARRIES & CASH

Another 16 year old who joined the Company in 1929 was Archibald (Archie) Hancock and soon after the Auxiliary Fire Service was formed at the beginning of World War II Archie joined as a volunteer. He was standing in for a colleague when the Clevedon engines were called to assist in fighting fires at Avonmouth docks in 1941 and was killed when a lone German plane returned to drop its bombs on the burning target.

Hale's Home Bakery was closed for the afternoon of Mr. Hancock's funeral and nearly 200 mourners attended the Parish Church for the service.

Norman Searle's father Bill started as the night dough maker then joined Ted Clothier as van salesman and is shown in the photograph below with his van and van boy Bob Warren in 1933. He worked for Hale's for 49 years and Norman himself retired from his position as Regional Sales Manager in 1984 after 46 years service.

Then came Mr. Hutchings who, as an expert sponge cake maker, became the chief 'sponger' and soon Mr. Rose joined the firm as a cake decorator.

He was affectionately known as Pop Rose to the young ladies he was later to train in the art of cake decoration.

Hale's Farmhouse Cake was not an instant success but after distributing several free samples for customers of shops in Clevedon and Portishead sales took off and it proved to be a winner.

To cope with a rapid growth in business the staff had soon increased to over 80 with 15 ovens in a well equipped bakery and 15 vans to deliver the goods. Soon Hale's vans were to be seen all over the West Country. They were selling 8,000 Farmhouse Cakes a week at 7 old pence each (just over 3p)! Dundee cakes were one shilling (5p) and 6 jam tarts for 5d. (2p).

In 1933 Frank Hale formed **Hale's Home Bakery (Clevedon) Ltd**. Production facilities on the site expanded as demand grew and he extended distribution of his products locally. He then had 200 employees and opened sales depots at Swindon and Totton (near Southampton). He was probably the first to recognise the potential of packaged cake in illustrated cartons for sale through outlets other than the traditional baker's shop.

The vans therefore were in constant use and the wear on tyres was found to be enormous so in 1938 the Company commissioned Goodyear to look into the situation. After inspecting and testing the vehicles they found 15 of the 28 vans with mis-aligned steering geometry and a large proportion of tyre pressures incorrect. Goodyear carried out all the necessary remedial work and trained one nominated member of Hale's staff at each site to be responsible for maintaining correct tyre pressures. Given the state of some of the roads at that time it was recommended that wheel alignment be checked once each month and thereafter there was a considerable improvement in tyre life.

The Clevedon Mercury of 29th October 1938 tells of an interview with Mr Hale when he reported that the company's daily output of all lines was 500,000 which included 10,000 Farmhouse Cakes, 15,000 Banbury cakes, 2,000 Sultana Cakes and four tons of slab cake! They were now making 30,000 decorated Christmas Cakes ready for the festive season.

The reporter observed the swiss roll making process where the ingredients were mixed and poured onto a slowly moving greased belt in a foot-wide strip. He saw the belt enter the oven and, through a peephole watched the strip turn from white to cooked brown. From the oven it passed under containers which sprinkled on sugar, then spread jam, after which the strip was cut into equal sized pieces by a rotary cutter. Only then was it touched by hand where nimble fingered girls rolled the sponge, wrapped each roll and packed them in cardboard boxes.

Swiss rolls were always hand rolled by girls; apparently men were completely hopeless at the task!

Meanwhile, underneath the railway arches in Holloway, North London, another small bakery had been developing, its name at first was Electricakes! However it was bought out in 1927 and the new owners, Messrs C.S. Johnston and H.S. Rowlandson, felt that a more homely name was required so they invented John Trent. John, because it was a good old English name and Trent because that was the title of a country estate near to the home of one of the new owners. John Trent therefore was another "man who never was" but people addressed letters to him personally for as long as the Company existed.

Quarries & Cash

In 1930 another group, Fitch and Son Ltd bought half the shares of John Trent and expanded the business in a new plant in Leyton. Distribution by an extended sales force was by open fronted Model T Ford vans, known to the drivers as 'pneumonia wagons'

Fitch & Son Ltd became The Fitch Lovell Group and acquired a number of subsidiaries including the Far Famed Cake Company.

By 1941 Frank Hale's health began to fail and he sold a majority interest to the Fitch Lovell Group.

The following year Mr. Hale died tragically at the early age of 49 but Mrs Hale continued for a while to operate the business with the assistance of a caretaker management visiting from London on a rota basis.

Growth continued through distribution in the southern half of the UK, then in 1956 Hale's commenced extension of its distribution throughout the whole of the UK. Depots were set up in Cheshire and Yorkshire in the North; Warwickshire and Wiltshire in the Midlands; Suffolk, Kent and Sussex in the South East; London; Glamorgan in South Wales and in Devon so the whole country could benefit from the output from Clevedon.

Sales teams were established at each of these depots and in 1957 for example, their wages were based on a fixed £3.00 per week plus a commission based on the value of sales up to a maximum of one shilling (10p) in the pound for sales over £600.00. A guaranteed wage of £9-10-0 (£9.50) was however set but it appeared to be a rare occurence for any of the salesmen to have to claim this. A top salesman could sell an average of £450 worth of cakes each week and when a Farmhouse Cake was around 20p retail and six jam tarts 10p that was a lot of cakes.

Top Salesman Award Eastern Area

Silver cups were awarded annually to the most successful salesmen in each region.

In 1963 the bakery was modernised and extended at a cost of £1.5m, and the substantial new facilities enabled Hale's to claim the most advanced bakery premises in Europe.

Facilities were included for the production of frozen foods but this unfortunately was too far ahead of its time because very few retailers had frozen food cabinets in which to store and display the goods.

Hale's Sales Challenge Cup

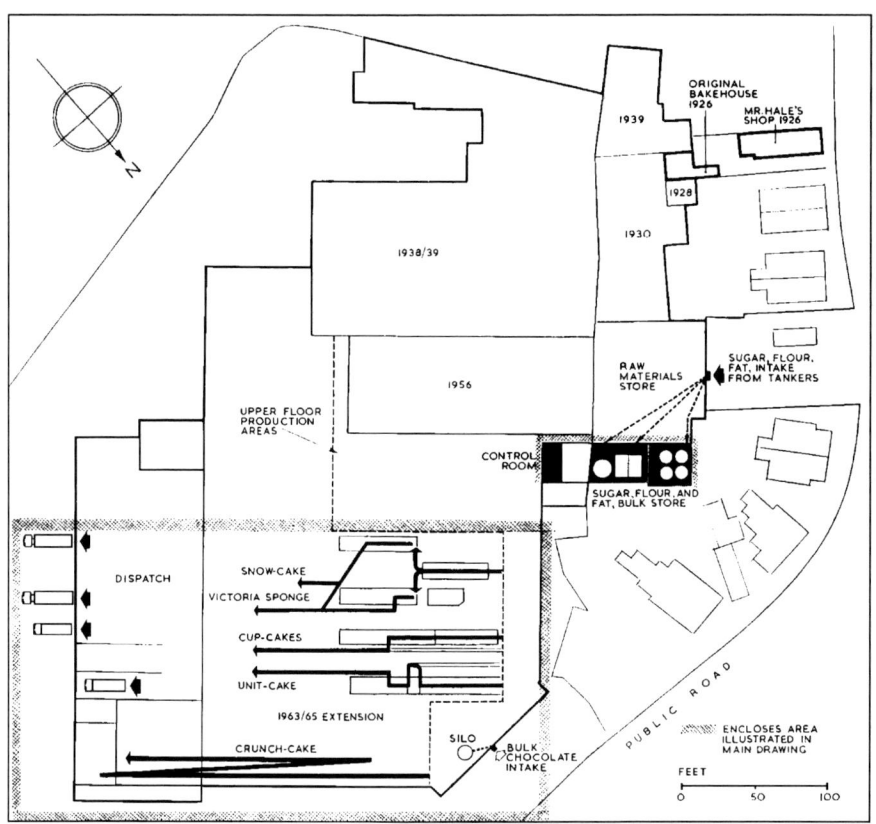

A simplified layout of the Clevedon factory in May, 1967, giving the approximate date of each extension. All the early dated areas were still in use at this time, and a number of the original employees were still serving the company.

A digression—

During the modernisation the fire escape steps from the old two storey building were removed.

As the old building was still in use the door to the now non-existent fire escape was nailed shut. However it had been normal practice in hot weather to have this door open for extra ventilation so the nails were unofficially removed.

Now Clevedon had a retained fire brigade where firemen were drawn from all walks of life and when the town fire siren sounded they downed tools where ever they were and made haste on foot, bicycle or car to the fire station to man the engine. One of the firemen worked on the second floor of the old building and, yes you've guessed it, on hearing the fire siren, forgetting the fire escape had gone, opened the door, stepped off into space and crashed through the asbestos sheet roof of the boiler house coke store below.

The roof shattered and he landed on the heap of coke beneath, rolled down to the floor, picked himself up, rushed past the startled stoker, got on his bike and was on his way in record time!

QUARRIES & CASH

To resume:—

In 1965 the merger of Hale's with John Trent Ltd took place and the Company became Hale-Trent Cakes Ltd. The Leyton bakeries were closed and the production centralised in Clevedon but with the sales areas merged to cover a large part of England.

Problems with obtaining ingredients with the quality required to maintain a satisfactory output of Hale's Farmhouse Cake resulted in it disappearing from the shops but it was soon to be replaced by Grannie's Cake which virtually swept the board over the whole country.

The development of Grannie's Cake is a story within a story and started when Mr. Rowlandson's son-in-law Norman Lambourne was shown a cake recipe his mother had found in her mother's recipe book. She had made the cake and found it excellent and suggested that the recipe be sent out to members of senior staff at the various bakeries in the group with instructions to each go out and buy a mixing bowl, all the ingredients and a cake tin and make an individual cake as a sample with a view to including it in the Group's output. This move was greeted with some hilarity and incredulity by the staff but, as Mr. Lambourne was a Director, the instructions were followed by 14 members and the resulting cakes sent off to his mother for assessment.

Percy Greenwood, who has recorded his experience of his attempt recalled that one instruction was that the oven door must not be opened during the cooking time and that one of the ingredients was Crosse & Blackwells Gravy Browning and it MUST be C & B!!. He said that when he took his cake out of the oven he was ashamed of it as a possible commercial proposition but sent it off as instructed. He was surprised to learn that his was one of the best submitted and was deputed to develop the production process, first at John Trent at Leyton then it was introduced to each of the bakeries at Hale's at Clevedon, and Far Famed at Poplar. When Leyton and Poplar were closed all the Grannie's Cakes were made at Clevedon.

The No. 1 Swiss Roll production line

Photo courtesy of North Somerset Museum

The cake tins were individually greased by hand, the mixture fed in then pressed down by hand and Demerara sugar from one particular producer in the Caribbean sprinkled on top. The Fitch Lovell Group bought the complete output from the sugar supplier each year so that no competitor could duplicate the crunchy sweet topping on the cake. The photograph shows the stacks of cake tins and them being greased ready for the mixture.

Staff greasing the 'Grannie's Cake' tins

The cakes were cooked in traditional gas ovens and then film wrapped to enclose each cake while still warm. It was intended to call the cake Mother's Cake but Rank objected because they had the name Mother's Pride registered for their flour. Rather than fight the issue it was decided to call it Grannie's Cake but then Meredith & Drew objected because they had Granny's Cookies. A compromise was reached where Meredith & Drew agreed not to make cakes and Hales would not make biscuits under the name Grannie's or Granny's! After the name was sorted out the new cake became even more popular than the Farmhouse Cake had been and was one of the best selling cakes in the country.

Its continuing fame was almost certainly because it continued to be made in the old fashioned way of personal observation of the mixing of 400lbs of milk, eggs, flour, fat, Demerara sugar and dried fruit to decide on when the mix was ready for the oven. This was carried out by Ray Small and Alf Hucker who with their many years of experience knew when the consistency was just right, something that could not be done automatically despite having the most up-to-date bakery equipment available. Then the 'hands on' treatment mentioned above gave each cake an individual character and quality was assured right up to end of Hales at Clevedon's because each week one cake was sent off to Norman Lambourne's

QUARRIES & CASH

mother for her to check and woe betide anyone who attempted to streamline the process!

In the case of almost all the other recipes used by Hale's, machines were programmed to complete their tasks within a preset time to produce the correct texture - including the 30 miles of sponge made each week.

In 1971 the Clevedon bakery had 12 manufacturing plants on the site using 3,000 tons of flour, 2,600 tons of sugar, 600 tons of dried fruit and 10 million eggs a year (some of them seagulls eggs I believe). It enjoyed substantial sales of a range of cartoned and film-wrapped products including jam tarts, fruit pies, slab cake, whole cakes (round and loaf), sponge sandwiches, Swiss rolls, flans, trifle sponges and crunch cakes.

Distribution transport was considerably improved by this time over the old Ford T and one of the more modern Hale's sales vans (Reg. PNC 157) was seen in the Marty Feldman film 'Every Home Should Have One'!

The proximity of the M5 when it opened in 1972 had prompted the evolution by Hale's of a unique form of cake distribution in the UK. Articulated lorries carrying up to 11 tons of cakes serviced some 250-satellite cake sales vans that distributed to nearly 20,000 retail and wholesale food outlets each week. The whole transport fleet travelled 2,500,000 miles every year.

There was a well-equipped vehicle maintenance department on the Clevedon site and it was from here that the maintenance of the hundreds of cars, vans, buses and lorries was co-ordinated throughout the U.K. The Clevedon premises housed production facilities, despatch department, raw materials and paper stores and it was the Administrative Centre for the whole company. The local sales operation, distribution, vehicles and research & development facilities were all housed on the Clevedon site, which employed many hundreds of personnel both full and part time, with over 200 sales personnel being based throughout the UK.

Special buses were run to bring staff into Clevedon from outlying districts in time for the start of each shift so good time keeping was automatic - well almost. There was also a staff bus to the mushroom farm at Congresbury and it was not unknown for a sleepy head on a cold, wet and misty winter morning to get on the wrong bus!

Cakes for special occasions were made to individual order, and decorated to the customers requirements no matter how bizarre or difficult. A brass band complete with trumpeter for a wedding cake, a cake in the form of a packet of detergent, Armed Forces Association Badges, all were produced with only 14 days notice required. When a Hale's employee married he or she was presented with a wedding cake by the firm. The number of tiers was related to the length of service. A one metre square wedding cake was made for a daughter of the Forte family.

Many of the social activities of the staff were regularly reported in a bi-monthly supplement in the North Somerset Mercury and included skittles, golf, cricket, football, holiday competitions, participation in the Clevedon Carnival, days out by special train from Clevedon, and the annual dance. Percy Greenwood the Assistant Production Manager suggested that there should be an annual dance within the bakery building but the proposal was turned down at first because it was believed that it would interfere too much with production. However after much persuasion and a promise to eat his boots if so much as an hour was lost Percy was given the go-ahead.

Clevedon Staff - 25 years service

Standing l to r: A Stone, T Bennet, N Hucker, J Carey, R Small, E King, M Carey, G Harris? R Osgood, M Powell, N Searle, B Watts, L Head, G Farndon, R Weids, R Law, C Coles, G Price, A Baker, W Reed.

Sitting l to r: T Oldman, G Tomes, G Stone, A Gill, R Renolds, R Small, G Tomes, L Stackham, K Jones.

After closing time on the Friday evening before the dance each January the Dispatch Department, a vast 25,000 sq ft hall was cleared of conveyors and packing cases by a team of volunteers and decorated ready for Saturday. Staging made from pallets for the bands, lighting, a 40 foot bar supplied by the Reading House, and of course lots of food made in the bakery kitchens made the Hale's New Year Dance an annual highlight for about 1,000 guests. Needless to say by the time the Monday morning shift arrived everything was back to normal, shipshape and Bristol fashion and Percy never had to eat his boots.

QUARRIES & CASH

The children weren't forgotten either as this photograph shows them at their Christmas party. Where are they all now? Who was Father Christmas?

Photo courtesy of North Somerset Museum

The Company continued to grow through the dynamic leadership of joint Managing Directors Fernley Parker and Gordon Salmon, drawing it to the attention of its larger rivals.

In 1973 Hale-Trent Cakes Ltd. was bought by J. Lyons & Company. Gordon Salmon took over as sole MD and he and the employees of Hale-Trent kept Lyons Bakery at bay through the very dynamic operation of the business. The Far Famed Cake Company was merged fully into the Hales operation with the closure of its bakery in Poplar, London. Ken Sydney who had joined Hale's at Clevedon in 1956, went to Far Famed as Production Manager, then returned to Hales at Clevedon as Production Director.

Production with a capital P - take the Jam Tart and Mince Pie lines, the completely automatic system could produce 10,000 per hour on each of two lines but this wasn't enough to meet the demand so a third line was added. Can you possibly imagine the organisation needed to have delivered the required amount of ingredients, the feeding of them to the mixing section, the baking ovens, the filling, wrapping, packing and shipping of 30,000 jam tarts each hour. Then think of an 8 hour shift, that's nearly a quarter of a million a day and that is only one of 12 production areas. To achieve all this, Tony Perrett ably assisted by Gordon Ling, led a dedicated team of maintenance and development engineers. Not only did they keep the factory running smoothly but they also constantly improved the efficiency of production with their inventiveness and ingenuity.

In 1981 the Lyons Board (part of the then Allied-Lyons, now Allied-Domecq group) restructured the European Bakery operations and Gordon Salmon became MD of the UK operations. With wholesale sales of £155m p.a. (Lyons Cakes £80m, Symbol Biscuits £40m, Hale's £30m, Frozen Cakes £5m), the UK was very strongly represented in the total Allied-Lyons European operation at that time. In Europe the group was represented by Panrico (Spain & Portugal), Hooimeijer (Holland), Hagemann (Germany), Picard (France) and Gateaux (Ireland). European sales totalled some £650m p.a. Hale-Trent produced products for some of those countries, as well as a small export trade to many parts of the world in its own right.

During the early 1980s the supermarket companies were consolidating and, as they grew, placed more and more demands on the companies supplying them in terms of service, quality and price.

By 1985 Ian Gazzard had moved from Hales to become MD of Lyons Bakery, Richard Turner taking over from him at Clevedon. Allied-Lyons Board came under very considerable pressure as the result of a huge error of judgement by one of its executives, and resultant profit pressures impacted on its operating companies. This resulted in the conclusion that future investment in new plant and buildings must be centred on Lyons huge (and under-utilised) manufacturing plant in Carlton, Barnsley, and the decision was taken to close the Clevedon plant and move all production to Barnsley. This closure was preceded by a merger of Hale's selling operations in the UK with Lyons Bakery, and rebranding of products into the Lyons brand.

The announcement of Clevedon's closure was met with dismay by the staff and the town in general because, as the largest employer in the district, its disappearance would affect a wide section of the population. However in the face of the inevitable the co-operation of its very loyal staff enabled the closure to take place on a phased basis from April 1985 into 1986. The site was eventually sold to Clerical Medical, the buildings on the site demolished and a brand new office building erected in its place.

In 1994 Allied-Domecq, as it now was, made a decision to withdraw from the food business. Through 1994 into 1995 Lyons Biscuits and Lyons Cakes were sold off, together with many other of their famous food and beverage businesses and the Hales brand disappeared from the shop shelves of the UK - 70 years on from when Frank Hale started at Clevedon.

Roy Girling

With very grateful and sincere acknowledgements in particular to Miss Iris Hutchings, Mrs. Lily Greenfield, Mr. Roy Osgood, Mr. Norman Searle, Mr Ken Sydney, Mr. Ian Gazzard, Mr. Alan Blackmore, The Clevedon Mercury and Mr. Nick Goff at the North Somerset Museum, W-s-M.

QUARRIES & CASH

Clevedon's Quarries

Clevedon is built on more hills than Rome* and the early builders of Clevedon did their best to level a few of them by creating 23 quarries in the 19th Century You will find remains of them all over the town where the builders had blasted away the various types of stone to clear spaces on which to build, using some of the stone they had extracted. There's limestone, Pennant sandstone, triassic conglomerate, dolomite — you name it and you could probably find it in one of the quarries in the town.

The knowledge and skill of the builders in the art of blasting would appear to have been suspect in some cases judging by the correspondence raised on the matter.

Here are some examples which express the concern of near neighbours to the activities of the blasters:

A New Freestone Yard

Letters to paper in April 1865 -

Sir,

Could you through the medium of the Clevedon Mercury allow me to call the attention of the Inspector of Nuisances to the fact that a portion of Victoria Road near the Beach is being rapidly converted into a freestone yard. Each day that passes tends to make matters worse. I have remained quiet for the past six months thinking that when the building opposite was completed there would be a cessation of the sawing etc. which make my mornings a misery and shortly, I am afraid, will be the cause of shortening my visit to this pretty little watering place. Last week I procured a copy of the local byelaws and there I find that the builders causing these things to be done shall be fined and pay for every such offence a penalty not exeeding five pounds, and in case of continuing the offence a further penalty not exeeding forty shillings for each day; after written notice of the offence from the said Local Board or other authorized officer.

Feeling sure that the inspector will look into the matter for me and the parties residing in the houses near, allow me to remain Sir,
Yours etc.
A Visitor

Letter May 13th

The new Freestone Yard

Sir,

Many of your correspondents have recently and justly complained of the nuisance ocasioned by the blocks of freestone being placed too closely at the side of Victoria Road and the complaints appeared so well founded that the surveyor actually took pains to remove the nuisance from one side of the road to the other. Where I contend that it is more damaging and unsightly than it was before. There is also the stone quarry adjoining my garden. To which I most earnestly draw the attention to those whose duty it is to keep a watchful eye upon all wrong doers. I have had my

63

windows constantly broken from the blasting of the rocks. Huge pieces of which fall with unerring precision upon my premises to the imminent danger of myself and of my family; and when I complain to the men working in the quarry I am simply told that "They will attend to it" and nothing more is done. The road dirt has also stood in heaps at the corner of Anglesea House since Christmas last. The rule is that it should be moved within forty eight hours of its collection, but this is left undone. Much has been said and written about the right man in the right place; but the little town of Clevedon must ever remain I am afraid with the stiff luck of having the wrong man in the wrong place.

I Am Sir

Yours Obediently

E Sargeant

And there's more!

This next letter probably refers to the small quarry on Wellington Terrace opposite the new Edgarley Court apartment block:

February 10th 1877

The danger of blasting

A letter was read from George Finzel Esq. of Wellington House, Wellington Terrace drawing attention to the danger to which he was exposed from the blasting going on at the Quarry near his house.

The other day a stone fell through the roof of the dwelling house, and a large number of stones, specimens of which lay on the Board table, flew through his night nursery window, his little boy had left the room but a few minutes before the stones came in, or the consequences might have been serious.

The quarry was being worked by Mr A Caple and the Board of Health. The unfortunate shot proved to have been laid by the Board of Health miner, although one of Mr Caple's workmen had managed to hit a chimney stack with a charge a short time before.

The Surveyor had stopped his men, as had also Mr Caple, and the Clerk was requested to communicate with Mr Day the owner of the Quarry, informing him of the danger to which the public were exposed.

June 9th 1877

The quarrying nuisance

A letter was read from Mr Davis, of Beechcroft, calling attention to the blasting operations carried out by Messrs. Shopland Brothers in Albert Road - a large number of stones had been hurled into his gardens, and neither life nor property could be considered safe. Mr Woodforde (the Clerk) informed the Board that a stone, the size of a hen's egg, had passed through the plate glass window of his son's residence, Elmhurst, at a point where only a few minutes previously a child was standing - had not the little one moved away he would undoubtedly have been killed, as the stone came like a cannon ball. Another member said that a quarry existed behind this row of houses, and Mr Hartree stated that an immense piece of stone was thrown into Rosemont, (next door to Elmhurst), smashing everything before it.

QUARRIES & CASH

It was a risk of life, limb and property both at the back and front, and the Chairman likened it to a bombardment, and expressed himself that it would be best for him not to let another quarry unless under the authority of the Board. The surveyor was directed to see the parties working the quarries.

The old Hangstone Quarry in Old Church Road is very evident and in Court Woods behind Clevedon Court is a quarry. Recent investigations indicate that the stone from it was used to build part of the Court.

The area on either side of Walton Road in East Clevedon was ripe for quarrying with the two hillsides to exploit. The 1830 survey reports a cottage and garden in an old quarry round about where the Calvary is now.

The quarry at the corner of Walton Road and Nortons Wood Lane was on Clevedon Court land and it would appear that when this reached its limit the blasters moved further down the lane and discovered Pennant sandstone. The Clevedon Parish Rates record of 1832 tells us that it was occupied by Messrs. Vickerage (Vicarage ?) and Pomroy from the owner, Sir A. Elton and was recorded as Coniger. The rate was 9d and the yearly value £3. In 1845 the working of the quarry came into the hands of the Baker family, Samuel first then John who seemed to be involved in it at least until 1891 where his name appears in the census as a quarryman. The quarry's name varied over the ensuing years being recorded as Cunagor; Pennant Quarry; Norton's Wood, then Conygar in 1891. It became the last working quarry in the town and is now notorious under its present name of Conygar Quarry.

If you have been walking in Court Woods you have probably noticed that there are lots of rhododendron bushes on the north side of the hill but none on the south side. The reason is that the northern side is sandstone and the southern side limestone and rhodo's don't like lime.

Geological studies indicate that the Pennant sandstone at Conygar Quarry is part of a fold which occurred millions of years ago and it is understood that the coal measures at Nailsea are part of the same fold.

The quarry men started to extract the hard blue-grey Pennant stone for buildings and roads. You can find it all over Clevedon in garden walls, cottage and farmhouse floors, the curb stones along the edges of pavements and some of it is in the Clock Tower in the Triangle. As far as is known, the last building project to use Conygar Quarry stone is the Senate House of Bristol University.

When used as flagstones for floors and paths the area to be covered was carefully measured and stones were then cut in the quarry from the quarried pieces so that when placed together would fit the required area. Each one was then numbered on the back using Roman numerals (all straight lines so easily chiselled out) and when delivered to site were placed in strict numerical order.

The stone when crushed forms a good non-slip road surfacing stone and this has been its recent attraction.

Ken Ball, one of the last people to work in the quarry in mid 1950 has described how the Pennant stone was found to be overlaid with lime stone as the quarry face was extended so that it was possible to extract both types of stone as required!

To cut the stone into blocks, first, steam driven reciprocating saws were used then, electrically driven circular saws, and the screaming sound they made could be heard all over the town. No noise abatement laws then apparently!

Alfred Ware has sent the following personal recollection of his fascination with the quarry when he was a boy 65 years ago:

> *"Boys who wanted to be engine drivers when they grew up had visions of journeys along tracks stretching into the distance. My hero, Harry Hiscock `drove' an engine which never moved, because it was the stationary one in Conygar Quarry.*
>
> *Resting on iron-rimmed wheels, the main attractions of this engine, for a young boy, apart from its tall chimney, the noise and its smells were the glowing fire box when this was opened for stoking and its great driving wheel. The latter was connected to a much smaller wheel on the air compressor by a flat belt several inches wide. When the engine was started up the compressed air produced was piped to the pneumatic drills to bore holes into the rock. These holes were later filled with the explosives used to blast the Pennant stone from the quarry face.*
>
> *The men who did this dangerous work appeared to have a safety rope secured to some point above them, but it was not possible to see much detail as unauthorised persons were not allowed anywhere near the area.*
>
> *When the sound of drilling stopped there was an ominous silence, but before the charges were detonated a clear warning was given to men working nearby. At the same time a man shouted "Fire!" from the road above my grandparents' cottage. Everyone then hurried indoors. This may have seemed to be excessively cautious, but it was surprising how far some pieces of rock were hurled by the blast, both into the woods and sometimes as far as the warren.*
>
> *Occasionally one came through the roof of my grandparents' cottage. My grandfather would then 'go along to see Jesse' (the foreman). I thought this to be a most bold thing to do, as Jesse had a rather forbidding appearance, but I realised in later life that the two men had probably known each other for years.*
>
> *After blasting came the hazardous business of prising free the great slabs which had been loosened, but still clung to the strata. A crane with a jib capable of reaching these work areas played a part in this.*
>
> *The total result of the drilling and blasting was eventually brought together on the quarry floor, then loaded into skips and pushed along rails to a point near the steam engine.*

QUARRIES & CASH

Secured to an endless cable, which ran between the rails, each skip in turn then began its run down the steep incline to the crusher, pulling up an empty one as it did so. The single track became a double one half way down to allow them to pass each other. The best place to observe this was from the footbridge, that carried the public footpath from the Warren to Nortons Wood Road, over the trackway.

The loaded skip came to rest on a platform about two thirds the way up the side of the crusher. The skip's locking catch was then released and the rock tipped into a hopper. The process of reducing the chunks of stone to the sizes required for road surfacing was both noisy and dusty. (An uncle of mine worked in and around the crusher plant for a time and I remember him stripping off to wash away the grime at the end of a working day).

The finished road stone could be released into a lorry or a skip waiting at ground level beneath the crusher. That stone loaded into skips was then pushed, on rails, across Norton's Wood Road to a position close to a braking mechanism. This was basically a large, open ended iron cylinder three and a half to four feet in diameter and three feet in length. It had gear wheel teeth around its rims and was mounted on a supporting frame, with a braking gear incorporated.

Conygar Quarry - Footbridge over tramway

The procedure which followed was similar to that used to move skips to the crusher with the weight of a full one used to pull up one that was empty, but on this longer run the skips were moving up and down an embankment built over a field, and ending up above some railway trucks in a short siding. The contents of the skips were then the tipped down into the trucks. When filled these were usually coupled behind passenger coaches of a Weston, Clevedon & Portishead light railway train and taken away in the direction of Portishead.

Lorries filled with roadstone had their loads assessed at the weigh-bridge, situated close to the winding gear and the office where Miss Anstey dealt with the paper work.

On the opposite side of the road, up a short, rough pathway was the shop where Jack the blacksmith kept all the cutting tools in good shape. He used a circular bellows operated by a crank handle to heat the coals and the steel chisels. We boys thought this was much more interesting than the ordinary bellows used in the local smithies.

In the midst of all this mechanisation was a group of men producing something entirely by hand. Known as bankers and working in an area close to the steam engine, they made flagstones and similar stone blocks using just a hammer and steel chisel. The clinking sound of their chisels seemed never to stop throughout the whole working day.

On or two things above the quarry had survived from days long past. Close to the cliff edge were the remains of a cottage which eventually disappeared as the workings were extended. I'm fairly certain that my great grandmother had lived there with her second husband. The other interesting things were two circular water tanks, enclosed in stone walls. These had supplied water to the cottages below. The pipes which carried it were to be clearly seen against the long abandoned cliff face.

Harry Hiscock eventually left the quarry company. When I last had a word with him he had found a new career at Portishead Power Station. As kindly and cheerful as ever he gave me a brief but vivid account of the great flashing and sparking which occurred when he regularly threw some main electric switches there.

I hope he was able to live out the rest of his active life somewhere in the world of the engineering he loved."

The quarry ceased as a commercial operation in the 1950s and then was used, among other things as a vehicle scrap and parts recovery depot until the late 1980s when some speculating optimists tried to start it up again as a working quarry.

After bulldozing a boundary bund, destroying some fine trees in the process they started work with a loud BANG which brought the local residents to their doors to see what was going on.

QUARRIES & CASH

Later explosions were more moderate but it would seem that the returns on the investment were not adequate and the firm went into receivership in 1992. Various attempts to reopen the quarry have been frustrated by the activities of local residents and the present plan is to build houses there. No doubt rockeries would figure highly in the associated gardens!

Roy Girling with help from Jane & Derek Lilly

* Rome is reputed to be built on seven hills but Clevedon has at least twelve: Back; Castle; Chapel; Church; Court; Dial; Hangstone; Highdale; Marine; Strawberry: Sun; Wains.

The stationary steam engine used to operate the stone carrying tramway (I don't think the lady is the regular operator, though!)

CASH

A Brief History of Banking in Clevedon

For readers who are unaware of the changes which occurred in the ownership of Banks in the 19th and early 20th centuries, present day takeovers give the industry a very stable appearance. I will take in turn, the four Banks which are represented in the town at present - March 2001.

Lloyds TSB

In 1862, the firm of Harwood & Harwood opened a private banking establishment at Holland House in Hill Road (now known as Handel House and the ground floor split into a hairdressing shop and an antique shop), premises built by Edmund Gurney in 1861/2 and which 100 years later were occupied by Walkers, the grocers. In 1877, Harwood & Harwood was absorbed by the West of England and South Wales District Bank, and when that failed in 1878, the business was taken over by the Wilts & Dorset Banking Company, which at about that time moved to the corner of Hill Road and Belle Vue Road, and was absorbed by Lloyds Bank in 1914. The business premises were altered over the years and extended into what had originally been the attached home of the Manager of the Bank.

In the Local Board of Health Minutes of the 1870s there are records of correspondence over a nine year period between the Local Board of Health and their Bankers (Messrs Harwood & Harwood) about a commission charge of £1:8:4. (or if you prefer, £1.42) made by the Bank, which ended in the Board's account being transferred to a competitor.

'The customer is always right' (of course) but on the other hand, bankers can be very dogmatic, so nothing has changed.

There is a story of there being a "well house" with a well beneath on what was lawn at the front of the Bank. Once a week, a pony was brought to the Bank to work the pump which raised the water from the well to a tank in the House. This operation could not be seen by the public, as at that time there was a high wall around the garden and a large elm tree which together made the Bank almost impossible to see from the business end of Hill Road, but in the early 1900s, the wall was lowered, the tree felled, the well filled in and the "well house" demolished in order to make the Bank more visible.

So there was a banking business on this site from 1878 until 1998 when Lloyds closed the branch, by transferring all business to their branch in the Triangle which had been opened as an agency from the Hill Road office in 1929 on the site it still occupies.

Lloyds Bank also have an office at Yatton which was opened as an agency from Hill Road, but that link has long since been severed.

QUARRIES & CASH

Barclays Bank

Barclays Bank opened its first branch in the town at Six Ways on June 1st, 1956 under the control of the Bristol Local Head Office; the address was changed to No.2 Linden Road in 1965, and Barclays occupy the same premises today. In January 1993, The Clevedon branch became part of the Weston - Super - Mare Group, now the North Somerset Group. The premises had previously been the printing machine room of the Clevedon Printing Company.

In recording the opening in 1956, The Mercury remarked that anyone remembering the old machine room would be amazed at the transformation, the walls being painted almost a duck-egg green, the counters and fittings in light oak, and white woodwork around the windows. The light fittings were white and modern, all making the room look even lighter.

With control from the Sixways branch, Barclays opened a sub-branch at 22-24 The Triangle on March 24th, 1975, premises which are now occupied by a shop selling linen goods. However, the Branch was a relatively short-lived venture, as it was closed on October 28th, 1988. These premises had earlier been occupied by a branch of Westminster Bank after that Bank had moved from No. 2 Old Street about 1967. Another sub-branch of Barclays Bank at Sixways was opened at 63A High Street, Nailsea on July 6th. 1970, which became a full branch at 134, High Street, Nailsea on March 15th. 1982. It is interesting to speculate why The Triangle sub-branch closed and why the Nailsea one proved to be a success.

❊ ❊ ❊ ❊ ❊ ❊ ❊

NatWest

This is not quite as straight forward as Lloyds and Barclays Banks.

(i) Hill Road

A branch of Stuckey's Banking Company was opened in 1874 at No. 49 Hill Road, premises which today are occupied by Eclectica, "a suitable house opposite Messrs Harwoods Bank, (at Handel House - see Lloyds Bank) belonging to our customer Mr. Lavington". On July 17th it was reported that "Mr. Lovegrove having offered us from September 29th. the premises .... at £50 per annum and three shillings and sixpence per week for cleaning the office. It was decided to accept the offer". In October 1877, another report - "This is now ready for us to go into and we hope to commence business in it during this month".

On March 30th, 1880 a site for a new building was purchased for £300 freehold and in May architects were appointed to build the new Bank for £1,650. This is the 'stand-alone' building on Hill Road between Dunscombes (the opticians) and The Regent and which after about 117 years, ceased to be a Bank on October 17th 1997, the business being transferred to the branch in The Triangle.

In 1909 Stuckey's Banking Company (and the Somersetshire Bank) was acquired by Parr's Bank and in 1918, Parr's Bank merged with London County and Westminster Bank to form London County Westminster and Parr's Bank which, in 1923, was mercifully shortened to Westminster Bank Limited. During 1968 the Westminster Bank and National Provincial Bank, (together with District Bank which had been a subsidiary of National Provincial for some years) announced their intention to merge. The operations of all three Banks were combined over the following 18 months and became National Westminster Bank from January 1st, 1970, and so these premises became known as National Westminster Bank - Hill Road Branch.

As Stuckey's Bank, the front door was in the centre of the 5 attractive arches, but a photograph taken sometime in the 5 years of London County Westminster and Parr's Bank (which name incidentally went from end to end along the front of the building), shows the front door having been moved to the present position - at the right hand end of the building. I wonder if the glass in the windows was changed every time there was a change of name - it all makes work for the working man to do!

(ii) The Triangle

London County Westminster and Parr's Bank opened at No. 2, Old Street in January 1920 (the premises where Mr. Bill Bryant had a gentlemen's outfitting business from 1977 to some time in 1988 and now the premises used by Palmer Snell the estate agents). The name of the bank was shortened to Westminster Bank in 1923 in line with the Hill Road branch and was managed from that office. The business moved to No. 22, The Triangle in about 1967 and on January 1st, 1970 on the official merger (see 'Hill Road' for details) became Clevedon, 22 The Triangle Branch. On July 19th, 1974 the branch closed, the business being transferred to the other branch of National Westminster Bank in The Triangle, just across the road.

The National Provincial Bank of England opened a branch in Clevedon on April 1st, 1903 at No. 15, The Triangle (also known at some time as No. 3, Selwood Place) which was the right hand half of the present bank - now known as No. 9 The Triangle, as a weekly agency (Fridays only - 11.00 a.m. to 3.00 p.m.) to the existing branch at Portishead. In 1918 the National Provincial Bank of England merged with the Union of London and Smiths Bank to become the National Provincial and Union Bank of England. This name was shortened to National Provincial Bank in 1924, and became National Westminster Bank - Clevedon Triangle Branch as described under the Hill Road history.

HSBC

Formerly Midland Bank

(1) Sixways

The very grand premises at the bottom of Belle Vue Road were opened on August 18th, 1924, with Mr. F. W. Hole appointed Manager. He had joined the Midland Bank in 1899, and came to Clevedon from Tiverton. By 1931, the staff had increased from the original two to six; Mr. Hole retired in 1942. In the Midland Bank Circular which announced the opening of their Clevedon Branch, amongst other notes, there is one to the effect that the exchange rate for French francs was 82 = £1. and today I see it is 10.35 = £1, how times change!

Of the Bank buildings in Clevedon, these premises must rank as about the most impressive and from what I have been able to unearth, have been subjected to much less change of ownership and less structural change than the others. I understand that before the building became a Bank in 1924, it was a surgery and the Doctor's house.

(2) Old Church Road

This Branch office to Sixways was opened in the early 1960s in the building until recently occupied by an estate agent on the corner of Lower Queen's Road and Old Church Road. It was a very small office, four or five people together in the public space would have felt like sardines (I am told). In September 1980, the Bank moved to its present (and much larger) premises No. 6, Old Church Road. In November 1984, control of the two Clevedon branches was reversed, that in the Triangle became the parent branch, with Six Ways becoming the Branch office. On September 27th, 1999, the Midland Bank nationally became H.S.B.C. (Hong Kong & Shanghai Banking Corporation), and so, another familiar name was swept from 'the High Street'.

Miscellaneous

Mention is made in "The Complete Clevedon Guide" dated 1879, of The Clevedon Penny Bank at the Village Hall, but I have no information on this venture.

It is interesting to learn that Hill Road was the place where the Banks became established in Clevedon, but now, sadly they have gone, whereas the agencies/ Branch offices down in The Triangle area have flourished. Is this a reflection of the business life of Clevedon as a whole in 2001? I hope not, but I do wonder.

On a point of clarification, a Branch office (or sub-Branch) would have had its own staff whose place of employment was at that office for the whole day. It would have its own book-keeping system, strong room, open and close its doors in line with current practice and to all intents and purposes be a separate branch as far as the public were concerned. However, an agency (either daily, weekly or any combination) would be staffed by a member of the controlling office with a guard. They would probably arrive in a taxi, and (experience suggests) usually at least five minutes after the office should have been open to the public, carrying cash for the day in a suitcase. The cash at the end of the day was taken back to the parent branch with the appropriate vouchers and all the processing done there. The hours during which an Agency was open were arranged locally and did not follow a set pattern.

It is amazing to remember that some of those offices had no adding machines or typewriters, and some, not even a telephone! Electronic calculators were unheard of, ballpoint pens were prohibited, fountain pens accepted but frowned upon, and steel nibbed 'dip' pens and blotting paper, the order of the day; and that was less than forty years ago.

Christopher Norrish

September 18th, 2001

Help was greatly appreciated from Mr. Paul Williams and staff at H.S.B.C. Bank in Clevedon, Jane Lilly, Mr. Bill Bryant, Mr. Norman Cudmore, Mr. Peter Ganniclifft and Mr. Lawrence Hagley.

Other Publications by Clevedon Civic Society

Clevedon History Trails
(with map and 3 walks)

Footpath Walks in Clevedon

Clevedon: From the Village to the Town
(The story of how the town developed during the nineteenth century)

Clevedon Past
(More studies of local history)

The Annals of Clevedon
(Further studies in the history of Clevedon)

Clevedon's Social & Industrial Heritage
(Further studies in the history of Clevedon)

Footnote

Referring to the chapter on Penicillin in Clevedon's Social & Industrial Heritage

Mr. S. E. C. (Sec) Read who was a trainee at Clevedon and who has now lost most of his sight, told of his memories to Peggy Tigwell who then recorded them for this footnote.

Mr. Read left school in 1939 aged 16 and joined the Dorchester County Laboratory - attached to the local hospital - as a trainee laboratory assistant. At 18 in 1941 he received his 'calling up' papers and was told by the Medical Research Council to join the Navy.

He then went on a course and passed as a Service Trained Male Nurse and was sent to the laboratory at Haslar Hospital in Portsmouth as a Sick Berth Attendant. The Navy decided that he hadn't had sufficient training so sent him to the Royal Navy School of Medicine in Clevedon. He trained at Clevedon to be a Laboratory Assistant and soon found that the man in charge, Chief Petty Officer Lemar was quite a strict disciplinarian but "a man that always looked worried". There were several Training Officers the main one being P.O. (Knocker) White who in his spare time played football for Clevedon.

The subjects taught were theoretical and practical aspects of Public Health, Chemistry and Bacteriology and in his final examination, Sec, as he was called,

R.N.M.S. Clevedon - July 1943

Back Row	John Bastable	John *(Plum)* Buttimer	Walter Stirrup	P. O. White *(Knocker)*	Ray Booth	? Palmer
Front Row		Stanley (Sec) Read	Reginald *(Reg)* Commander	Muriel White	John Sedman	

obtained a Pass with Distinction. It was a 22 week course completed in January 1944. Mr. Read has always felt thankful to the Navy for such a good basic training. The importance of hygiene was very much instilled into the trainees and tropical medicine also was included in the curriculum.

The building at No.5 Elton Road was being used to produce vaccines for all the Armed Forces but the trainees were not told of the research into penicillin at the time. He afterwards discovered it was used on troops on wounds as a powder and in fluid form and given as injections.

There was a room into which they were never taken and so being a nosey kind of fellow he got in to have a look what was going on. He found that it was completely fitted out with narrow shelves filled with bottles full of mould - then he was caught! He later found that they were filled with a by-product of the local brewery and a mould added to grow on the fluid. This produced quite a rough penicillin which was later refined by Parke-Davis.

The trainees were all around 18-20 years old and were billeted in various places in the town. Sec, with two others were over a shop in the Triangle. The owners lived over the shop and were extremely good to them,- but can you imagine the giggles of three 19 year old lads living above a Spirella corset shop!! The photograph shows a group of the trainees.

Mr. Read finished his working days in the Laboratory at the Weymouth Hospital as a Senior Lab. Technician and while visiting the Dorchester Lab. met up with Peter Norris who was the Clevedon schoolboy who joined them at the Clevedon Lab. as a messenger boy.

With acknowledgements to **Peggy Tigwell**
Local History Group

Acknowledgements

In addition to the people acknowledged by the authors at the end of the individual chapters there are many others, including the authors themselves, who have helped to bring to light a wide range of local knowledge and the Local History Group appreciates the time and effort taken by all in helping to put on record some more of Clevedon's history.

There must still be a lot more information about people and events which are part of the development of our town and, as our Group Chairman mentioned in his introduction, we will be very happy to receive all contributions which will help to put on them on record.

Call Rob on 01275 877038 to start the ball rolling for the next book!